The Legacy Workbook
for the Busy Woman

*A Step-by-Step Guide for Writing a
Spiritual-Ethical Will in Two Hours or Less*

Breaking the Silence: Weaving Blessings and Words of Wisdom for Future Generations

RACHAEL FREED

MinervaPress, Minneapolis

Published by MinervaPress, Minneapolis. For more information, please call (612) 558-3331, or visit our web site at www.life-legacies.com.

First Edition: 2005 ISBN 0963779540
Second Edition: 2012 ISBN 978-0-9817450-1-5

Printed in the United States of America

09 08 07 06 05 8 7 6 5 4 3 2

Book design: Stephanie Billecke
Cover design: Christopher Kirsh
Cover Photo: Djerba, Tunisia, El Ghriba Synagogue Olive Tree by Patty Shapiro

Acknowledgments

This book was spun and woven by many hands.

— Laurel Thatcher Ulrich, *The Age of Homespun*

My deep gratitude and sincere thanks to all those named and unnamed who contributed their passion, ideas, voices, and love for legacy work, and for the writings shared that enriched the Virtual Legacy Circle portion of this book.

"Daughter of Two Houses," © Janie Breggin Braverman, appeared in Being Jewish, Fall, 2004; "The Death of Jacob," © Ruth Brin, appeared in *Harvest: Collected Poems and Prayers,* Second Edition, by Ruth F. Brin (Holy Cow! Press, 1999); "Where Did It Go?" © 2003 Ethelyn Cohen; "Tatiana Safranova, 1912-1970" © 2003 Dennice M. Gooley; "Grandmother's Legacy" © 2003 Laura L. Hansen; "A Letter to My Descendants," © 1998 Denise Linn in *Sacred Legacies* (Ballantine Books); "My Mother's Hands" © 2004 Sue McGuire; "These Things I Love," © 2004 Vicki Pearson; "Connecting Up," from *Kitchen Table Wisdom* by Rachel Naomi Remen, M.D., copyright (c)1996 by Rachel Naomi Remen, M.D. Used by permission of Riverhead Books, an imprint of Penguin Group (USA) Inc.; "We've Woven You a Blanket" © 2003 Sue Renwick; Excerpt from "Loss" © 2002 Susan Tilsch, appeared in *Women's Lives, Women's Legacies* by Rachael Freed.

Blessings: Dona Billey-Weiler, Barbara Crist, Judy Dunlap, Lisa Gunther, Laura Hansen, Barbara J. Levie, Bill Marsella, Lyn Mowafy, Gretchen Scheffel, Susan Tilsch, and Sister Rita Von Holtum for the Jacob blessings created with her family education class at St. Philips Catholic Church in Litchfield, Minnesota.

Domestic Arts: © 2003 Ethelyn Cohen; © 2004 Lisa Gunther; © 2004 Janet Kenney; © 2004 Barbara J. Levie; © 2003 Sue Lewis; © 2004 Mary Meinert; © 2004 Joan Munzner; © 2004 Vicki Pearson; © 2004 Jane L. Toleno; © 2004 Laurie White.

Letters: Anonymous & © 2003 Cynthia Anderson; © 2000 Stephanie Czerniecki; © 1997 Bonnie Denmark-Friedman; © 2004 Judy Dunlap; © 2003 Mary Small; © 1971 Irene Stillman; © 2004 Susan Tilsch; © 2012 Claire Willis.

General Contributors: Anonymous & © Nancy Blanchard; © Julie Bolten; © Barbara S. Crist; © Judy Dunlap; © Laura Hansen; © Sue Lewis; © Janet Kremen Thorkelson; © Susan Tilsch.

An exhaustive effort has been made to locate all rights holders and to obtain reprint permissions. If any required acknowledgments have been omitted, or any rights overlooked, it is unintentional. Please notify the publisher who will rectify any omission or error in future editions.

Contents

Introduction

I felt an urgent need to pass to my daughters not only my dreams for them and my values, but also the idea that these are the most important legacies I have. And it is crucial that this legacy be in writing, for writing is itself an act of faith.

— Wendy Schornstein Good

Blessed by working in legacy circles with many women since the publication of the first edition of *Women's Lives, Women's Legacies,* I heard expressed over and over, a need for a resource less demanding of time. Many women, because of their busy lives, need a guide to document their legacies in a time frame that better fits the demands of their lifestyle.

My challenge was to provide a book addressing the exploration of our histories, our selves, and our values within a limited time frame without being superficial. My goal was to provide a down-to-earth practical workbook without sacrificing the spiritual essence inherent in legacy writing. And finally, my hope was that this book would communicate the power of women's voices and provide the skills necessary for women to express our experience and our wisdom in writing. With assistance from many women legacy writers, I present you with the Second Edition of *The Legacy Workbook for the Busy Woman.*

Several themes are woven into the workbook. One focuses on how both ordinary and extraordinary each of us is. Many women, although attracted to the idea of passing on a legacy, fear that their ordinariness makes them barren of anything worth transmitting. Rabbi Laura Geller writes about the holiness of each of our stories. Paraphrasing Deuteronomy 30:11–14, she suggests that like the one who chops wood and the one who draws water, the one who drives car pool and the one who makes dinner has a sacred story

A self is made, not [only] given. It is a creative and active process of attending a life that must be heard, shaped, seen, said aloud into the world, finally enacted and woven into the lives of others.

— Barbara Myerhoff

Courage in women is often mistaken for insanity.

— anonymous psychiatrist about Alice Paul, a suffragist, in 1917

The opposite of language is silence. Silence for human beings is death.
– Joyce Carol Oates

Each of us is the distillation point of a great funnel in time that consists of the history, culture, and evolution of our species.
– Denise Linn

It is time for the world to hear women's voices, in full and at last.
– Teresa Heinz Kerry

May all women realize the grandeur of their origin.
– Helena Roerich

that connects each of us to our own tradition and future. I hope you will find your sacred essence as you document your legacy, expressing both your ordinariness and your extraordinariness.

Perhaps the most important theme is about breaking the silence that has held women hostage through the ages. There are inspiring quotations, chapter titles, and purposeful reflections to support you finding courage and language to tell your loved ones and the world who you really are and what matters most to you.

One legacy circle participant wept, realizing how little of her talents and power her mother had expressed during her lifetime. Most of us didn't really know our mothers or foremothers. We have our memories of them in their roles as mothers, wives, workers. Few of them shared who they were beyond or behind those roles. When they're gone, we experience deep regret and unending yearning to know who they really were: what mattered to them, what and whom they loved and valued, their disappointments and pain, their successes and joys, and their hopes and dreams for us. The first chapter of this workbook addresses this need by exploring who our personal and cultural foremothers were, and by gathering the legacies they passed on to us.

The need to know others, especially those from whom we came, is the mirror image of our own need to be known, heard, seen. Chapter 2 focuses on an aspect of our feminine essence often ignored in our busy world. It will give you a fresh perspective about who you are, what is meaningful in your life, and it will clarify your contributions.

We can conjecture that those who come after us will either be enriched by the gift of our written legacies, or be yet another generation left without roots, a sense of connection, or belonging to foremothers, family, and community. Armed with a sense of who our foremothers were and who we are, we begin in chapter 3 to articulate the verbal portraits, the values and wisdom, we want included in our spiritual-ethical wills.

In chapter 4 we address the preciousness of our lives, and our thoughts about our mortality as seen through the lens of legacy. And in the final chapter,

chapter 5, we gather and weave what we've collected in the first four chapters to write legacy letters to loved ones and to future generations.

In the course of this workbook you will be provided with the patriarchal history of the ethical will of tradition. We grew up in a culture and at a time when women's stories and experience were neither recorded nor valued. But now we live at a time when our loved ones and the world need our values and our wisdom. Thus the need for women to transform the traditional ethical will to make our unique contribution to future generations.

Please don't mistake this will of history, stories, values, wisdom, and love for a legal will. It is neither a legal will, which distributes your material estate, nor is it a living will, a medical and legal document detailing your end-of-life directives.

I want my children to know the values I hold most dear, which do not change no matter the times
– Marian Wright Edelman

Suggestions for use

First read the chapter's introductory material, meant to stimulate your thinking and engage your feelings. This is followed by suggestions for personal reflections and directions for a related writing exercise.

After each writing exercise, you are invited to think and write about your process. Process writing may include your feelings and thoughts: about what you learned by writing, about the content you explored, and further questions based on your experience with the exercise. A guide to thinking in a "process" way is included to help you differentiate between this writing and the exercise, which has a different focus.

Process writing adds an invaluable component to our self-knowledge, thinking, and writing. Master teacher, Stephen D. Brookfield, expresses the value of critical self reflection: "Critical reflection . . . is a method to stay current, honest, and open about uncovering our habits, assumptions, and biases, and looking at how those are expressed in [our] content and dynamics," and "Not to be critically reflective is to think that our actions don't have much effect," or "to think that what you do when you show up . . . makes little difference to anyone or anything."

Only at the end of forty years do we begin to understand that even our life stories are sacred . . . and that God has been involved all along.
– Lawrence Kushner

When can we be equals?
When people speak and make
room for others by listening
well. When we use silence, to
affirm rather than betray
ourselves or others. When
human differences are
welcomed, respected and
treasured as our finest resource
and allowed to form, inform,
and transform us all.
– Jane L. Toleno

We will surely carry our scars
with us for the rest of our days
on this earth. But our struggle
for life will lead us to a deeper
understanding of ourselves and
of our place in this world.
It will lead us toward insight,
toward blessing, and
toward God.
– Naomi Levy

When you have completed the exercise and process writing in the chapter, you arrive at the Virtual Women's Legacy Circle. What is it? Why in a time-limited book such as this is this included?

The legacy circles that I have been privileged to guide have been rich in many ways, but perhaps the most important is the gift the women give each other when they share their writing in the safety of the circle. Two ground rules of the circle are: we don't analyze any woman's writing (this is neither a therapy nor a support group); we don't critique any woman's writing (this is not a writing group). It is unusual in any setting for women to be listened to – without interruption, without questions, critiques, or analyses. Legacy writers thrive as they are listened to with unconditional acceptance.

The women listening also gain from the experience. They learn experientially to appreciate the uniqueness and the connections among us. Each woman articulates her own experiences, stories, and history in a unique way, and yet the themes – the struggles and suffering as well as the celebrations and successes – connect us beyond our differences. Not only do we come to appreciate the diversity represented by the writing in the legacy circle, but our memories are prompted, our ideas of what we want to write are expanded as we listen to each other.

When women evaluate their experience of participating in a legacy circle, most say they wish there'd been more time – to hear each other's writing. Although you sit alone with your workbook, women who have written before you have generously shared their writing with you. Reading them, you have the virtual experience of being part of a legacy circle. (Please note that the last page of this workbook contains your invitation to participate in a new virtual circle, a collection of women's wisdom.)

You may be tempted to read what others have written before you write, but I suggest that you follow the order of the chapter. Do your own reflection, writing, and process writing before you read what others have written. Why? So that you don't intimidate yourself or short circuit your own creativity by comparing yourself with what others have written.

On the other hand, the legacy circle exists so we can learn from each other and benefit from the sacred diversity that every legacy circle contains. In our time, borrowing or copying from another is considered cheating, even plagiarism. But during the Renaissance, young artists were apprenticed to masters; they learned their craft by copying. In legacy circles women often hear another woman's writing and realize that they've experienced something similar, and may decide to write about it themselves. This is one of the advantages of doing legacy work in a circle of women.

Please note that at the bottom of each exercise page, you are invited to make additional copies for your personal use. If, after reading the writings in your virtual circle, you want to write again, or you decide to repeat an exercise at a later date, you can. Always date and save what you write, so that you have a record of your spiritual/creative evolution.

We live today in a world starved for authenticity, for traditional values made new, and for love that is real. Creating a spiritual-ethical will – an enduring document that communicates your history, who you are, what you value, and how you want to be remembered – is a way to respond to those needs that celebrates your life, and makes a real difference for the future.

We stand here together at the genesis of a sacred journey, one that links us to our selves and others, to past and future generations. May your journey be rich and fulfilling, and may it be a gift beyond measure. May all your legacies be blessings.

RACHAEL FREED

We are all in this together and our writing and reading one another is a powerful comfort to us all.
– Julia Cameron

There seems no way but the way of candor and curiosity to be remembered well by the people I care about. Some cold evening in their middle age, perhaps a grandchild or two will sit by the fire and read something I've written. In this way, the way of words and imagination, we'll cross time and space together.
– John Burns

*May your history
and your voice
be freed from silence.*

CHAPTER ONE

$\mathscr{B}$reaking the Silence

Discovering the Legacies of Our Foremothers

Legacy writing is one part self-discovery and finding your own voice. The other is passing your legacies on to your loved ones. We grew up in a culture and at a time when women's stories and experience were neither recorded nor valued. Today it is urgent that we bless our loved ones, the world, and future generations with our values and our wisdom.

Welcome to this workbook and to the sacred task of documenting your legacy. We'll begin by exploring two subjects you'll need as preparation for writing your legacy. One is to have a sense about your unique identity and values, to know who you really are.

But first we'll examine how we're connected to our personal and universal history. Having a sense of the legacies passed down to us by our foremothers provides roots and the experience of belonging.

We ache for the stories of our history to fill a void we often find difficult to define. Few of us know our foremothers, or understand the lives of the feminine ancestors who created our families and the traditions of which we are a part. Our goal in this chapter is to recover those legacies, and to reclaim our feminine history and heritage.

Exploring a Foremother

To begin: Consider your foremothers, your feminine ancestors, and then choose one of them who you would like to know better. She may be a grandmother or great grandmother, an aunt, or another relative. Even if you know little or nothing about her, choose a woman about whose life and experience you are really curious. Or choose a woman to whom you feel particularly connected, especially if she seems mysterious. You don't have to know at this moment why you feel attracted to her. She may be a foremother you never met, a woman whose life was lived before you were born.

When you've made your choice, write her name in the space provided, and spend no more than five (5) minutes compiling a list of the facts you know about her. It's okay if your list is short.

Consider what you know and what you don't know about her. Here is the place to jot notes about your assumptions about her, what you *believe* is true about her. The second list may include stories you were told about her, or rumors whispered about her in your family, but you have no real proof of their authenticity. Spend no more than five (5) minutes recalling and recording your assumptions about her.

Considering what you know for sure about your foremother as well as the sense you have about who she is, illuminates the gaps in your knowledge, the places where you still have questions about her life and values and how you are connected to her. Asking questions and remaining curious, more than seeking the "right" answers, often yields meaning. In the third space, record at least three questions you wish you had answers to about her, her life, her legacy to you.

Exploration of One of My Foremothers

Date of writing:

_____ , my _____
(her name)   (designate her relationship to you)

FACTS I KNOW ABOUT MY FOREMOTHER'S LIFE:

_____

_____

_____

_____

_____

_____

_____

_____

_____

_____

MY ASSUMPTIONS ABOUT MY FOREMOTHER:

MY QUESTIONS ABOUT MY FOREMOTHER:

Grandmother's Legacy
by Laura L. Hansen

Grandmother Hansen,
(Mimi, to us),
Wrote poems
To her children –
Beatrice, Bernhart,
Ove, Claude,
John, Milo, Bernice –
Poured out her heart,
Gave instruction, Thanked God.

Sometimes she mailed
Those Poems
In letters drenched
In love and stretched
By loss.

Sometimes
She stuffed them
Into the backs of drawers
Where they mingled
In silence with dust
And string and the snow
Of powdered old pills
And little tangles of hair
Pulled loose from a comb.

Lord only knows,
How many she threw out.
Emotional treatises, all
Rhymed and crumpled,
And lost. To her,
They were as necessary
And unseemly
As the Kleenex
She tucked inside
Her sweater's sleeve.

Her daughters rescued a few,
Folded inside letters,
Pulled from yellowed envelopes
Bearing stamps of only
A few cents. Others
Were lifted from inside
Those untidy
Dresser drawers
When the girls were
Cleaning out the house.

From these
They made up slender
Hand-bound books,
One for each family,
Less than twenty pages
Each. A lifetime saved.
A lifetime lost.

You've examined the facts and your assumptions about your chosen foremother. You've asked yourself what more you want to know about her. You realize that she has given you a legacy: perhaps a positive quality, perhaps some unresolved issue from her life. Here is a guided visualization to help you to recall and reclaim the legacies she has passed on to you. Reflect on the following and then write for no more than fifteen (15) minutes. Be sure to date your writing.

Arrange yourself so you are comfortable where you are sitting. Close your eyes and focus on your breath, following its natural rhythm . . . in and out. Notice that with each inhalation you are more in touch with yourself, you feel more centered and relaxed, and with each exhalation you let go of the distractions around you.

Imagine that you are going back in time to the place where your ancestor lived. Give her a moment to appear. . . . See her in your mind's eye. . . . Observe everything you can about her: her age . . . her gestures . . . the way she carries herself . . . her facial expressions and demeanor . . . what she is wearing, even how she smells. Notice her physical surroundings. Be aware of the qualities that make her who she is, both ordinary and extraordinary. . . . Observe how she is personally affected by her circumstances . . . her culture . . . her time in history. Be aware of her life struggles and life lessons. . . . What is she most proud of? . . . What are her greatest disappointments? . . . Who or what is she afraid of? . . . Whom does she love and who loves her? . . . What are her regrets and what does she wish she'd done differently? . . . What values did she teach her children by the choices she made and the way she lived . . .

Imagine that you can go back in time to where she lived. . . . Step into her clothes and into her shoes. Take on her posture, gestures, demeanor. . . . Wear her feelings . . . incorporate her thoughts . . . embody the qualities that make her unique. . . . Experience what it is like to be her, to live her life. . . . become her.

See yourself sitting at a table with pen and paper. You pick up your pen to write a legacy letter through time and space. This letter will include what you want the future to know about you . . . your hopes and dreams . . . your struggles, satisfactions, achievements . . . your regrets and fears . . . your loves and joys . . . your values and ethics . . . all that matters most in your life. . . . You'll conclude with a specific legacy meant only for her.

Now, open your eyes, pick up your pen, and begin writing. You may find that tears and strong emotions, hers and yours, accompany this writing. Keep writing and breathe deeply. . . . When you are finished, set your pen down, breathe deeply, feeling maybe for the first time seen and known, at peace having passed down your legacy.

Memory is often an effort to get acquainted with the stranger that was you a long time ago.

– Joan Didion

Without memories a race has no future.

– Denise Linn

A long time ago I expected you and I would be different. But no. The daughter must finish the mother's work.

– Carol Edgarian

My Legacy from My Foremother   Date of writing:

Dear _____, I want you to know who I am, and I have a legacy to give you . . .

_____

_____

_____

_____

_____

_____

_____

_____

_____

_____

_____

_____

_____

_____

Much love, _____, your foremother.

Processing

Processing is a term used in the workbook for you to take stock of your experience reflecting and writing. Your process writing will probably not appear explicitly in your legacy document, but it may clarify your values and deepen your insights, thereby contributing to your spiritual-ethical will. The following suggestions may help you get started:

Writing this letter may have stimulated strong emotions, even tears, as well as new thoughts and connections. Be sure to return to yourself in this time and place. Some or all of what you wrote may please you; some of it may be troubling. Recognize the special power and gift of receiving legacies from a feminine ancestor who you may never have met. As you write about your experience, check what you trust and what feels right.

What specific legacies did your foremother leave to you? Had they been expressed before or did this exercise break a long family tradition of secrecy or silence? How has your connection to your foremother changed because of this writing? How does a relationship with her clarify or deepen your roots? How does it add to your experience of having your own special place in your family?

Reflect on how receiving this legacy can affect your sense of yourself in this period of your life. Consider ways in which it may influence the legacies you want to leave your loved ones.

My mother's mother died in the spring of her years, and her daughter forgot her face.
– Leah Goldberg

I cannot have a future 'til I embrace my past
– Debbie Friedman

My mother wants me to know what happened, and I keep every detail of what she tells in my memory like black beads.
– Eva Hoffman

Process Notes: After the "Foremother Visualization"

The process was a strong experience. I feel like my head is a jumble of memories – a warm, familiar sort of longing to be together again.

This was a profound experience because I have not thought too much about her.

I'm not a writer, so putting ideas on paper is hard. This was an emotional experience for me. It brought tears to my eyes as I wrote. She is the symbol of the "rock" in our family and I had so little time with her.

I have such a full heart after communicating with her. I remember & do practice the most important values she taught – education and giving to the poor. This visit will remain in my heart forever.

Easier than I thought it would be; Did I truly write what she would have written or what I need to hear from her? Far greater appreciation today than ever before.

I felt like she spoke through me today and often guides me in my life – mostly without my being aware of it. If she were alive today, I would get to know her better and ask the questions that I have.

I felt relaxed and at peace. I feel more connected to my grandmother, and I now have my own grandchildren. It helped me to realize many of the values she taught me that I had forgotten came, in part, from her.

Actually it felt quite comfortable to be her. Perhaps that is because my father always said that I was "just like her." It made me stop and feel the sadness that I never knew her.

I'm surprised that the connection happens, and that I chose E_____ to connect with. This letter seems real – I could really feel how close and terrible the community in must have been for her, especially getting a divorce in those times.

Process Notes

Daughter of Two Houses
by Janie Breggin Braverman

It was a Christmas gift from my mother – a Christmas gift from a long-time lapsed Lutheran woman to her Jewish daughter.

I grew up in a house without God. In my teens, I searched for God in the charismatic Christian campus ministries. In my twenties, I sought God in the great outdoors, in the mountains of Colorado where I grew up, went to school, and married for the first time. In my thirties, I saw God in the faces of my children.

Then in my forties, I walked into a synagogue for the first time, for the bar mitzvah of the son of a friend, and came home to the faith of Abraham, Isaac and Jacob, Sarah, Rebecca, Rachel and Leah.

The day of my conversion was the first time in forty years my father had set foot in a shul. My daughters beamed from the second row and my son bounced from seat to seat in the back. My mother didn't come.

That gift from my mother had been carefully wrapped in red paper with white snowflakes, snowmen and candy canes. No Star of Bethlehem, no wise men, no cross. No "Merry Christmas," no Christ. No problem.

She means well, my mother, I have come to understand that over the years. Not merely that she means me no harm, but that she actually means me well. It has always been hard for her to show that. It has also been hard for me to see.

The paper crinkled as I opened the gift. Fresh paper, without the softness of recycling, gently frayed at the creased edges. I never minded the reused paper. I used to think she did it because she was cheap. Now I like it because, whatever her reason, it seems to me that she walks gently on the earth as I begin to think gently of her.

It is a sepia portrait of Julia McKee, later Julia Wingo. She is young, eighteen perhaps, but the photo is old. In the upswept hair, tight bun, high collar and closed gaze, you see nothing of the spirited young woman who was to become my great-great-grandmother.

The photo is a reproduction, a delicately retouched copy of the fragile original my mother found among my grandmother's things after her death ten years ago. It is framed in an oval of dark oak.

"Who does she look like?" my mother asks.

Dave, my oldest brother, gapes.

"She looks like Robyn," I say. Robyn is my niece, Dave's daughter, twenty-two and on her way to law school in Chicago. She looks like Rachel, I think. Rachel is my daughter, eighteen and on her way to college in California.

Dave turns to look at me. My mother looks disappointed, but it's not the look of disapproval and disappointment I've seen before. Law school? How are you going to pay for that? Or: You're pregnant . . . and getting married? Well, you're too old for me to tell you what to do. Or: Religion is a crutch.

Instead it's a look of confusion – as if maybe the portrait isn't of who she thinks it is.

Dave shakes his head. "Janie," he says to me. "She looks like you."

The portrait could have been me. Same high cheekbones, same delicate face, and same sometimes opaque eyes – the ones that say I don't feel like sharing myself with you. Same face as Robyn, as Rachel, as me. . .as my mother. Genetics run deep.

I wonder how my Scots-German mother felt, giving this likeness of the women in my family, giving it to her Jewish daughter at Christmas.

How can I help her find ease in my home, where the ketubah from my second marriage hangs on the wall, where my shelves are filled with Chanukiot, Kiddush cups and Sabbath candlesticks, where a mezuzah marks every doorway?

She came to my wedding, the year after she gave me the portrait, but she did not come to my bat mitzvah last year. How can I tell her that my conversion was not an act of betrayal – that although my soul is Jewish my maternal bloodline is still hers?

How can I tell her that the faith of my father and my other great-great-grandmothers called me? Called me home to God and my father's people, but did not call me away from her.

I wonder how my mother feels when she looks in the mirror and instead of seeing her seventy-four year old self, sees the Jewish face of her forty-nine year old daughter. I wonder what she thinks when she looks at me.

The portrait now hangs in my upstairs hallway. She is really quite beautiful. Julia McKee. Robyn. Rachel. My mother. And me.

Tatiana Safranova, 1912–1970
by Dennice M. Gooley

The poet spoke of Zambacco and how she was her muse, her mistress, of how she becomes her voice through her poems.

You could say I had an epiphany. The discovery that a muse is what has been missing for me.

I realized that you have always been there, waiting, waiting for years. I have been too frightened to listen, not wanting to believe.

I have heard it said each of us is born with a song to sing, and left unsung it is silenced forever when we die.

You left no song, no art, no letters, and no childhood photos. No record of your birth, no record of your marriage. Only a passport, nine children and a death certificate.

Are you to be my muse, my inspiration? If so, I call you Tatiana, Mother of the Muses.

Within your womb lay all your voices, the beautiful voice that could sing of your heroics, leaving Brynsk. Coming to America, sixteen and alone – makings for an epic.

There is the voice of love for the man who never knew the meaning. The well-pleasing voice and the voice of the songstress who knew tragedy too well.

You should have been the central dancer – whirling – twirling the song of life, with your hair flying luxuriant and life just blooming. A voice that should have risen to the heavens, but you died with all the many sacred songs unsung.

Today I sing to you and for you. It is my prayer that your songs will be sung through me. That your legacy will not die with me but live on in the hearts of all who hear.

Tatiana was my paternal grandmother. I remember seeing her only a couple of times; she lived in Michigan and we lived in Minnesota. The last time, I was perhaps 10–12 years old. I was the first child, of her first child. It is as if we were connected at some other level – call it soul or spirit. It was never spoken. We looked like twins – especially our hair. Dark like mine, hers went nearly to her knees. I recall the thrill of brushing it when she let it down.

She spoke broken English, and when excited would break into Russian, and when very excited to a local dialect. She represented bravery, this woman forced to leave her home to create a new life. She escaped certain death in Russia from pogroms and persecution.

This letter/poem is part of a trilogy about my grandmother.

Your Virtual Women's Legacy Circle

Women in "Women's Legacies Circles," respect and appreciate each other's diverse experiences and values. They report being most moved by hearing what other women have written. Being listened to without interruption or critique is significant for most of us. We rarely have such a sacred gift in our daily lives. Even women coming to their first circle feeling shy or lacking confidence become eager to read their words and ideas. Listening turns out to be the glue that adheres circle communities of legacy writing women.

When I wrote *Women's Lives, Women's Legacies,* I wanted to simulate the experience. Women willingly shared their writings so that those who couldn't participate in a circle would have the opportunity to read the rich variety of stories and wisdom. Although it wasn't a perfect solution, women's writings and inspirational quotations do encourage readers to recall and record their own forgotten memories, to express how they are simultaneously ordinary and extraordinary, to appreciate their uniqueness, and to experience feeling intimately connected to a community of women that transcends time and space.

When I began *The Legacy Workbook for the Busy Woman,* women continued their generosity. Here and in each chapter of the workbook twenty-first century women join *your virtual* legacy circle. Imagine them sitting with you and sharing their writings.

Every act of listening . . . is an act of ordinary love that creates community where there might be chaos.
– Robert C. Morris

A story is truly great when you realize that you're not hearing just the story of the person telling it to you – you're really hearing your story.
– Marc Gafni

If we . . . go speechless, the stone dropped into the well will fall forever before the answering splash is heard.
– Faye Moskowitz

Legacy Letters from Foremothers

Dear Mary Eileen,

Today I want to share my sadness with you, as well as my hopes for you.

So much that I wanted in my life – as a young woman, I was full of enthusiasm and excitement – never came to fruition. I felt alone and different, neither understood nor respected. Part of that was the increasing distance between me and my children. They were intent on fitting in, becoming Americans, and they poked fun at much that I cared about. And my husband, your great grandfather, was a powerful man plagued with anger and alcohol, like his father before him. Nevertheless, he became a model for the boys, and the girls adored him.

I felt old before my time, like I was the receptacle holding all the grief and loss for everyone in the family. Life was hard. I worked long hours caring for nine children who rarely cared about me. They left prairie life for the city as soon as they could. I didn't have the strength to weather it all. At some point I just gave up and became resigned to loneliness and the death of my dreams.

But you must not give up. Let your dreams transform you – don't let the inevitable losses of life destroy you. May you have new and powerful dreams, and may your dreams come true.

– Your Great Grandmother, Mary

My Birth Mother

FACTS:
1. She lived in New York City and had me there on April 24, 1945.
2. She was of legal age.
3. She was a tall, statuesque blond.
4. She gave me up for adoption.
5. Her whereabouts are unknown to me.
6. She gave her name as Lillian Goertz, also known as Lillian Stirling.
7. She named me Ann Stirling.

ASSUMPTIONS:
1. She wasn't married to my birth father.
2. She was scared.
3. She wanted to keep me, but couldn't.
4. She was determined to move ahead with her life.
5. She thought about me often.

MY QUESTIONS ABOUT HER:
1. What circumstances resulted in you giving me up for adoption?
2. Did you ever marry and have other children?
3. Did you ever try to search for me?
4. Are you still alive?

HER LETTER TO ME:
My Dearest Daughter, I have so many dreams for you. I hope that you will be adopted by people who I would have chosen to be your parents if I had been able to pick them. I hope that they are well-educated, and that you have the opportunity to learn, to read, and to travel. I hope that you have inherited my love of music and the arts. I wish for you good health, close friendships, and a life with someone who loves you for yourself, and who cherishes you. If you choose to have them, may your children respect and adore you. May your grandchildren have special memories of wonderful times with you.

I wish you a life of purpose; a life lived to its fullest; a life with no regrets.

The only regret I have is that I will not be the one who will be at your side to teach and guide you. I will always love you.

PROCESS NOTES:
I have something important to say. Writing is a comfortable way for me to convey my feelings to others. Writing made me feel validated. Writing this letter from her was a very emotional experience for me, even after all these years.

Connecting with an Archetype

Even after making contact with a family foremother, many women still feel alienated from their history. Perhaps you've been disconnected from your personal roots because of adoption, immigration, family estrangement, abuse, or slavery. Yet each and every one of us has our place in the generations. We all belong. Weaving your way back to the beginning of recorded history, to an encounter with a feminine archetype, may be the thread that can bind you to history and roots, to a sense of belonging.

Western archetypes from the Bible, our Judeo-Christian source of family, include women whose stories and situations feel related to ours. There we find stories of real women who struggle with silence, neglect, and abuse similar to our own. A connection to one of them may give each unique one of us the commonality and comfort of belonging, of being a part of a larger human family.

With the same method we used to connect with our own feminine foremothers, we'll explore Dina of Genesis. "I've never heard of her! How could I feel connected to her? Who is she?" you ask. Dina is the daughter of Jacob, great granddaughter of Abraham and Sarah. Dina's mother is Jacob's first wife, Leah (sister of Jacob's second and loved wife, Rachel).

Dina's Story

The Bible (Genesis 34) tells us that Dina went out to visit the daughters of the land of Shechem. The prince of the land, Shechem, son of Hamor the Hivite, saw her and took her and lay with her by force.

Being strongly drawn to Dina, daughter of Jacob, and in love with the maiden, he spoke to her tenderly. So Shechem said to his father Hamor, "Get me this girl as a wife."

Jacob heard that he had defiled his daughter Dina. Since his sons were in the field with his cattle, Jacob kept silent until they came home. They came in from the field, distressed and very angry, because Shechem had committed an outrage in Israel by lying with Jacob's daughter.

And Hamor spoke with them, saying, "My son Shechem longs for your daughter. Please give her to him in marriage. Intermarry with us; give your daughters to us, and take our daughters for yourselves. You will dwell among us, and the land will be open to you; settle, move about, and acquire holdings in it." Then Shechem said to her father and brothers, "Ask of me any brideprice as well as gifts, and I will pay; only give me the maiden for a wife."

Jacob's sons answered – speaking with guile because he had defiled their sister Dina – and said, "We cannot do this thing, to give our sister to a man who is uncircumcised, for that is a disgrace among us. Only on this condition will we consent; that you will become like us, that every male among you be circumcised.

"Then we will give our daughters to you and take your daughters to ourselves; and we will dwell among you and become as one people. But if you will not listen to us and become circumcised, we will take our daughter and go."

Hamor and his son Shechem were pleased by their words. They went to the gate of their town and spoke to their fellow townsmen, saying, "These people are our friends; let them settle in the land and move about in it, for the land is large enough for them. We will take their daughters to ourselves as wives and give our daughters to them.

"But only on this condition will the men agree to dwell among us and be as kindred: that every male among us become circumcised as they are circumcised. Their cattle and substance and all their beasts will be ours, if we only agree to their terms; they will settle among us." All his fellow townsmen heeded Hamor and his son Shechem and all were circumcised.

On the third day, when they were in pain, Simeon and Levi, Jacob's two oldest sons, brothers of Dina, took their swords, came upon the city unmolested, and slew all the males. They put Hamor and his son Shechem to the sword, took Dina out of Shechem's house, and went away.

Like everyone ever born who goes through sudden, defining loss, women find themselves faced with the question: 'Who am I when I am no longer who and what I was?'
– Joan D. Chittister

What women need is the opportunity and the validation to name and describe the truths of our lives.
– Adrienne Rich

The impulse to find one's context, one's place in the galaxy is a basic need . . . that central element in the human soul.
– Barbara Kessel

The other sons of Jacob came upon the slain and plundered the town, because their sister had been defiled. They seized flocks and herds, everything inside the town and in the field, all their wealth, all their children and their wives. They captured it all as booty.

Jacob said to Simeon and Levi, "You have brought trouble on me, making me odious among the inhabitants of the land, the Canaanites and the Perizzites. My numbers are few, so that if they unite against me and attack me, I and my house will be destroyed." But they answered, "Should our sister be treated like a whore?"

Dina: From Silence to Legacy

Dina, named only six times in this story, is never mentioned again. That the Bible is silent about Dina after she was "ravished" by Shechem and "avenged" by her brothers doesn't mean we have to be. Consider the legacy we receive from Dina in the twenty-first century if we allow her to remain shamed, invisible, and silent (or silenced).

Whether you read the biblical text as a religious or a literary document, Dina's story is as painful and difficult today as then. It raises issues for women that have not changed significantly in the last 3500 years. Her suffering and silence mirror our own.

Who is unfamiliar with sibling rivalry and competition for favor in her family? Who among us has not been unprotected, neglected, or betrayed by her mother? By her father? Who has not grieved estrangement and loss of family and the loss of life hopes and dreams?

Who among us has not been in a situation in which we had no choices, were powerless to make decisions in our own interest? Who has not felt terror about survival? Who, fearing loss of love and acceptability, has not silenced herself? And who among us has swallowed her integrity in the silence of anger or shame?

How common is it to be demeaned, used, or abused by men? Who among us has not felt owned, like a piece of property or a token of another's success? Who has not questioned her worth as a woman? Who has not ached to be seen and heard? Who has not hungered for respect for who she really is? Who among us is not imploded with unspoken feelings and thoughts?

Is there a woman who doesn't yearn to live a life of meaning, feel her life matters, and that she can make a difference? Perhaps most painful of all, who among us has not at some time felt forgotten by her God?

And so it was with Dina, the archetype of the ravished, betrayed, and forgotten woman of Genesis: alone, excluded from her community, and silenced. Now you, in the twenty-first century, have an opportunity to give Dina the voice she never had.

Dina's Legacy

Imagine that you are traveling back to Genesis, to Dina's home in Canaan. Be aware of her family situation. Consider how the events and circumstances of her time define her. Reflect on her struggles and life lessons, her personal strengths and limitations. Whom does she love and who loves her?

Take a moment to imagine yourself in her tent. Slip into her sandals – and her soul. Become Dina and give her a voice to speak her story and her values – perhaps to members of her family, to her God, or to women of our time.

Use the letter format to weave words to leave Dina's legacy. Write for no more than fifteen (15) minutes. You can of course revisit earlier reflections and writings anytime. Returning may allow you to explore feelings, deepen memories and insights, clarify values, catch omissions or expand upon an idea. Be sure to date your writing and take time to process your learning.

To remain silent is to collaborate in the erasure of our past.
– Robert Krell

It is only the cruelty of truth, speaking it, shouting it, that will save us now.
– Alice Walker

Blind rage, helpless rage is rage that has no words – rage that overwhelms one with darkness. And if one is perpetually without words, if one exists in the entropy of inarticulateness, that condition itself is bound to be an enraging frustration.
– Eva Hoffman

She must learn again to speak starting with I.
– Marge Piercy

Dina's Legacy

Date of writing:

Dear _____, even after many generations of silence, I have much to say and a legacy to give . . .

_____

_____

_____

_____

_____

_____

_____

_____

_____

_____

_____

_____

_____

Dina

Processing

Here are some thoughts to stimulate your process writing:

Consider the value of reaching back to the archetype of a biblical woman to connect with women generically, and specifically to feminine issues that are millennia old. (Note: If you are interested in further connections with the oh so human women of the Bible, see chapter 2, "Discovering Sarah," in *Women's Lives, Women's Legacies*. (Sarah was Dina's great grandmother, who died without words. Her silence too may have been a legacy left to unnamed generations of women.)

Observe ways in which Dina's life circumstances connect to your history and that of your familial foremothers.

Consider the significance of silence. Notice which of your voices are silent (your angry-voice, your child-voice, your creative-voice, your fearful-voice, your loving-voice, your powerful-voice, your parental-voice, your spiritual-voice). When do pressures for silence come from within you? When from outside you? Are there situations when silence is of value, is useful, even preferable? How has silence affected your life and your desire to be an honest legacy writer?

My mouth and the words I say with it are mine and no one can take that away. I can't write like Dostoyevski or Henry Miller. I write like myself. I have to.

– Natalie Goldberg

Process Notes

Dina's Legacy

Dear Daughter,

You are loved. You are an extraordinary soul. I wish for you to be noble and kind and honest to all you live with. But refrain if you can from being silent.

Have the courage to change the attitudes of some. Be strong-willed as well as soft in nurturance. Tell others of your dreams and curiosities. I loved watching bread rise and so loved the aroma from our earth oases. The sun always warmed my body and soul and brought amazing change to our earth. Flowers and greens fed me and I brewed up some great medicinal remedies. I made soothing teas for our women's circles in our Red Tent moments. This you should know and more, my dear important girl. Love, your un-silent mom

Dear God,

See me Dina standing alone, without support from my father, my brothers, my mother, my aunt . . . all believing I had been defiled and their response to me was to make me ever after invisible.

God, that hurts. I don't want to be invisible. Why wouldn't at least You speak to me, send me a sign or a dream, to give my life meaning? What is my gift to the future? What is my legacy to our people, as tribe, as nation . . . there is no report of a child coming from my loins, so what purpose do I serve? What were you trying to teach through me? Do you realize that you left me a child, a victim, a woman without a voice and without choices and thus without meaning?

God, speak to me.

God, give me my voice.

God, give me a purpose for living.

God, give me a blessing, like you did the rest of my family.

Dear Father Jacob and Women throughout time,

First to you, my father: I must tell you that what Shechem did in raping me, a woman he didn't know, is forgivable, and I have forgiven him. But being excluded from your blessing on your death bed was a deeper wound. How could you bless my brothers, who were murderers and ravished women themselves, and treat me as though I were dead?

I will not be silenced. I will not disappear. I will speak, and I will bless you. God, forgive my father his weaknesses and his favoritism. And God, let my words be heard so that I send a legacy to all women through the generations.

Raise your voices — acknowledge your fear and then speak and write — vote with your voice and the written word. Be strong. Speak your truths. Do not let your times, your culture, your faith, your family, shut you down. Your humanity is at stake. Speaking makes you fully human — a woman of worth. By speaking you and I will be remembered and redeemed. Dina

Dear Aunt Rachel,

Why oh why is there not a tribe, a good luck 13th tribe named for me, sister of the twelve brothers, for all the women who stand alone — dishonored by community, because they are unmarriageable, by reputation or by choice. We needed a tribe, a safe place of refuge, as do women in every age.

And I'm angry at you, Aunt Rachel, mother of the people, the one lauded through time for your tears and compassion for children and barren women. You never cried your tears for me, your own niece, who would also be barren because her brothers stole her honor and marriage-ability, her future, her very life, and threw it in a pit, deeper than the one they threw Joseph in, since he got out and found a glorious place in history.

I ask you, Aunt Rachel, could God have loved my stepbrother Joseph more than He loved me? Your niece, Dina

Dear Father Jacob,

You have been a disappointment to me, and I'll tell you why. First, you never even tried to understand me in relation to Shechem. You didn't stand up for me when his father came to see you, nor did you protect me or my reputation, nor did you ask me what had happened. You never knew whether I loved Shechem and wanted to go with him, or whether they used me to try to take advantage of your success building a family and a flock.

Actually, I don't remember ever having much to do with you, or rather you with me . . . was that because I was a girl baby and child? Was it because I was Leah's daughter, and you preferred Rachel?

Your betrayal wounded me deeply. I recovered from being with Shechem; I recovered from the shame of what my brothers did, but I never recovered from the invisibility that you cloaked me in – how different from the cloak you gave my step-brother, Joseph – the most visible person in the herd of sheep, the most visible brother of all my twelve, the most visible man, except for Pharaoh, in all of Egypt – and I, i was never mentioned again.

How can I describe the pain of invisibility? I wondered if there was any worth for me having been born, or even to exist. Who would want to name their daughter for me, a victim rendered invisible by her family from the time of becoming a young woman as beautiful as my Aunt Rachel, my grandmother Rebekah, and my great grandmother Sarah. Most people don't even know that you had a daughter. There are no songs about me, unless one counts one verse of "I've Been Working on the Railroad." Maybe it would have been best if I'd just gotten on a camel caravan and left this family forever!

Dina, your only daughter

Dear Women of the 21st century,

    After many years of wandering, so wounded by my experience of abuse, made so small and powerless by the men who were making all the decisions in my life, I realize I can be silent no longer. I must tell my story. I believe now that one can find one's voice even if one has lived many years silenced. Silence does not have to be *forever*.

    I wish now I had stood up to Jacob and not allowed my marriage to be arranged. I wish I had screamed louder and kicked harder when I was being ravished. I think somewhere inside me I thought that I didn't have a right to say "no," that I didn't have a right to control my life.

    I have asked myself often why I didn't tell my story sooner, what kept me locked in silence over these many years. I feared that no one would understand what I had to say. I was afraid that I would be mocked and made to feel to blame or foolish, but I realize that the response to my words doesn't matter. I am no one without my voice. I can't live with myself if I don't let myself and my voice exist in the world. I can live with myself at the end of the day when I have spoken my truths, my feelings, and my values. It almost doesn't matter how they are received. Dina

Before you leave the discovery of the power of connection to your familial foremother and Dina, a word about what you've accomplished thus far.

Congratulations on empowering yourself by giving the past a voice! You may have just written for the first times – from your heart – as an adult woman. Now you can dismiss your fears about writing. Reclaiming an aspect of your familial and cultural history, previously shrouded in silence, takes courage and creativity. Weaving words for your foremothers and giving them voices is a milestone for you too.

You can never again believe that critical voice inside you; you know, the one who says, "You have nothing to say, and besides, you can't write." You've just proven to yourself that you are capable of expressing important values, no matter your prior confidence or educational background.

And you've practiced all the writing tools you'll need to write your spiritual-ethical will. You've written question-and-answer lists, process notes, free-style reflections, and legacy letters. You've used your imagination, intuition, and creativity to engage in the age-old tradition of writing Midrash.

Midrash literally means "investigation" or "exploration." Its purpose is to deepen understanding of sacred Scripture in its time, and make it relevant in our own. Lawrence Kushner, spirituality scholar, suggests that Midrash "is the writing that sprouts up in the spaces between the consecrated words of Scripture. Somewhere between commentary and fantasy, Midrash imagines . . . emotions and personalities utterly beyond the Bible's words. . . . *In so doing begins the sacred task of spiritual renewal.*" (italics mine)

Midrash helps us to realize that our own lives are sacred too. Rabbi Laura Geller proposes that, "As we tell our own stories we often discover the divinity that is present in our lives. And if we listen carefully, we hear our stories as part of the cosmic . . . story."

We nurture and strengthen ourselves making connection and community possible as we include ourselves in the 'cosmic story.' The wholeness provided by a legacy from our foremothers, mythical and our own, gives us the courage to value our own stories. We, like the bigger-than-life women

To be able to give, one has to possess, and we possess no other life, no other living sap, than the treasures stored up from the past and digested, assimilated and created afresh by us.
– Simone Weil

Why does anybody tell a story? It does indeed have something to do with faith, faith that the universe has meaning, that our little human lives are not irrelevant, that what we choose or say or do matters, matters cosmically."
– Madeleine L'Engle

Learning about your family heritage can free you to change the future.
– Monica McGoldrick

Stories have to be told or they die, and when they die, we can't remember who we are or why we're here.

– Sue Monk Kidd

of history, have a unique and sacred story, and a need to have our lives make a difference.

We began this chapter with the goal of connecting with our roots to give us a sense of belonging. Reclaiming and valuing the history and stories of our foremothers is an essential step to know and express our own. Hearing our foremothers' voices, we recover ours.

Dina exemplifies elements we all share from our common cultural past. She stands as a model of the profound loss of self that results from being silenced, from within or without. Exploring her story and the story of one of our family foremothers was a necessary leg of our journey from the historical and spiritual exile of silence to reclaiming our roots and our voices.

Armed by and nurtured with the legacies from our historical foremothers, we now turn to the present. There our work will be to harvest an aspect of our own essence, explore its meaning and value, and connect our every day lives with the divine and cosmic story.

*May you delight in the
power of the inner world
of hearth and home.*

CHAPTER TWO

$\mathcal{B}$reaking the Silence

Embracing Our Everyday Selves

Rediscovering Domesticity

Recalling and reclaiming the legacies from the lives of our fore-mothers brings us closer to wholeness in ourselves. With our roots entwined with their strengths and their voices, we bring a fresh perspective to the exploration of our values and who we really are.

Women's success and power have been defined by patriarchal standards in our society. Women are honored when we succeed in a "man's world." Hear the voice of Maria Mitchell (1818–1889), the first woman astronomer in the United States and the first woman named to the Hall of Fame of the American Academy of Arts and Science. Her words encouraged women to develop their powers: "A sphere is made up of not one, but an infinite number of circles; women have diverse gifts, and to say that women's sphere is the family circle is a mathematical absurdity."

The twentieth and twenty-first centuries shine with courageous stories of women struggling for the rights men held exclusive: suffrage, what's beyond the corporate glass ceiling, and equal wages for equal work, to name a few. I neither dismiss those struggles nor do I take the freedoms our fore-mothers won for us for granted. But neither do I want to diminish women's contributions of the past and the present. It is women who create and main-tain family and home, women who transmit the culture's history and the spiritual values – cornerstones of civilization.

In recent decades we've ventured far beyond the family circle, perhaps so far that we've inadvertently lost something valuable. Many of us were eager to expand beyond the drudgery, the routine, the lack of appreciation we found in the work of hearth and home. We didn't realize what it really meant to define ourselves as being "just like men." When we continue to accept that model, we compromise ourselves and unwittingly pass on this legacy to our daughters and granddaughters.

We know that there's more to us than our right and responsibility to speak and act in the outer world. But how to right the balance? To be whole, we need to reclaim the feminine: our bodies, our passion for beauty, our compassion as mothers – of our own children and all children on our planet. As we recognize the complex skills and sensitivity required to nurture and protect, to express our love and passion, we begin to shift the balance in ourselves, to feel our worth, and to exercise feminine power to contribute to the future of culture and civilization.

In this chapter we'll explore this often ignored topic with the goal of finding meaning in "women's work," which we'll define as creating and maintaining the inner world, the home, and the family.

Greek mythology honored these feminine qualities by creating Hestia, the goddess of hearth, home, and temple. She was the eldest child of Zeus, the first of the twelve most important Olympian gods and goddesses. Her symbol was sacred fire: a fire which was the source of light, warmth, and safety. Fire, essential in the everyday world of homemaking and mothering, also represented spirit, the light of internal meaning, the core of being.

My Body

I stumble when I try to think about my body as a sacred vessel housing my thoughts and my soul. I would love to be comfortable with this statement, to feel proud of my body . . . so I ask myself: How has my body served me? In what ways do I feel good about it? What are my body's special gifts? And these are my thoughts:

My body has given me signs to help me know myself. It tells me when I am full, when I am tired, when I feel passion to another, when I am afraid.

My body is wonderfully athletic, coordinated, and strong. It allowed me to be the fastest runner in my grade, even among the boys, through third grade. It allows me to enjoy and express my woman self in all sorts of individual and team sports.

My body has a gift of energy and stamina. It has allowed me to stay up all night writing term papers, to manage 15 hours of driving in a day across country alone, to have the strength to go to work on three hours sleep after dealing with children's illnesses, aging parents' crises, or traumas to precious pets.

My body has allowed me to feel beautiful and desirable in sex, to reach powerful orgasms, and to conceive children easily.

My body safely housed my growing unborn children and allowed me to miraculously birth them. It gave me the perfect breast milk for my children's nutrition.

It has allowed me to grieve fully with flowing tears and deep body-breaking sobs. It has allowed me to laugh and taste and hear and smell and touch and smile.

With a deep breath, and a true belief, I feel a new appreciation for my body, which has served me extraordinarily well.

Like Dina of Genesis, Hestia was made invisible. Most of us have never even heard her name. Hestia, the eldest goddess, was replaced in the Olympian pantheon by Dionysus, the youngest of the major gods. No paintings nor statuary honored Hestia or her sacred world of home and hearth. We don't know why this happened, but her disappearance is a legacy affecting all of us still today. Just knowing that there was a time and place in history when the inner world of women had a place of respect empowers us to reclaim that part of our birthright and heritage today.

Author of *Small Graces,* Kent Nerburn, writes: "If we should be so lucky as to touch the lives of many, so be it. But if our lot is no more than the setting of a table, or the tending of a garden, or showing a child a path in a wood, our lives are no less worthy." Each of us, living our ordinary lives, wants to experience that our lives matter, and to know the divine spark of light within us.

We can right the balance and realize Hestia's true legacy. We can experience with pride and delight the sacred nature of hearth and home. Then, in addition to our other values, we can bequeath this feminine legacy to future generations of women. (Note: For those interested in additional reflections and writing about mothering, feminine sexuality and spirituality, see chapter 6, "Woman, Mother, Sexual Being," and chapter 7, "A Woman's Spiritual Journey," in *Women's Lives, Women's Legacies.*)

Changing Dishes for Passover
by Rachel Naomi Remen, from *Kitchen Table Wisdom*

". . . You have never seen so many dishes, pots, knives and forks, and pancake turners. It all seemed really pointless to me, but it was so terribly important to Herbert and I was terrified of making a mistake and ruining things for him. But a really strange thing happened. Sometime in the middle of setting up things, I was standing by myself in the kitchen with my arms filled with the everyday milk dishes, looking around me desperately for some shelf room to be able to seal them away. Every shelf was full. I remember thinking, 'Where am I going to put these daily milk dishes?' and suddenly I was not alone. I had a very real sense of the presence of the many women who had ever asked themselves this very ordinary question, thousands and thousands of them, some young, some old, in tents, in villages, in cities. Women holding dishes made of clay and wood and tin, women dressed in medieval clothing, in skins, in crudely woven fabrics and styles I had never seen. Among them were my own grandmothers who had lived and died in Warsaw before I was born.

"In that same instant I also knew that if the human race continued, there would be women dressed in fabrics I could not even imagine, holding dishes made of materials not yet invented, who would be standing in their kitchens facing this same problem. Women who had not yet been born. They were there too. In the blink of an eye, alone in Herbert's kitchen, I was in the company of women across more than five thousand years. And too, at that very moment all over the world there were women asking themselves this very question in every human language, 'Where do I put these daily milk dishes?' And I was among them too.

"Well, Rachel, I almost dropped the dishes, I was so surprised. And it is hard to put it into words, but this was not just an idea, it was more like a happening. I had this vast perspective. I knew myself to be a thread in a great tapestry woven by women in the name of G-d since the beginning. You would think this would make you feel small, but it didn't. I was a single thread, but I belonged, something I had never experienced before. For a few seconds I had a glimpse of something larger, not only of who I am but Whose I am. It only lasted for a second, but I can remember it very clearly. I feel changed by it."

From Silence to Meaning: Reflecting On Domesticity

How can we accept and appreciate ourselves if what we do daily is meaningless, insignificant, without value? Jean Shinoda Bolen, MD, contemporary author of *The Millionth Circle,* suggests that "tending to household details is a centering activity, a means through which a woman puts her house and herself in order. . . . What she does pleases her and absorbs her. . . . As she sorts and folds laundry, irons or cleans up clutter, picks and arranges flowers, prepares dinner, or puts her closet in order, she is totally in the present moment."

If you're of the generation of stay-at-home moms and homemakers, what domestic activities do you find meaningful? If you're of the boomer or younger generations, how do you handle the contradictions inherent in the desire or need to work in the outside world and the longing or lack of inclination to spend your days in the domestic sphere?

What domestic memories do you have of your foremothers as they lived their lives in times different from today? How are these memories universal? Consider your connection to them and their generations. Which of the domestic arts do you think may connect you and your generation to the generations yet to come?

In all honesty, examine your present attitude about domesticity. How does/did domestic work define your value in others' eyes, in your estimate of yourself? How has your attitude changed on your journey through the cycles of life from childhood to the present?

Which of the domestic arts were significant in your development? Which taught you about your self, provided you with the ability to express a part of your essential nature? Which gave you practical skills, aided your independence, expressed something uniquely you?

Consider the qualities inherent in the domestic arts, and those in which you are, in varying degrees, gifted or limited: entertaining, creating beauty, a delicious meal, a hospitable environment, a safe haven for children. What domestic activities do you do today because of habit or a sense of obligation, and which of the domestic arts do you engage in as a choice that prompts your passion? Note any regrets about what you've done or not done.

Are their specific domestic arts which led you to understanding your authentic and unique self? How is/was your homemaking supported by extended family, friends, or faith community? What advantages and disadvantages do you experience when you work alone or with others?

Legacies of the Domestic Arts

Use the template on the next page to make a list. On the left side, record those domestic activities that you particularly enjoy, like, or find fulfilling or empowering. On the right side, list the domestic activities that you have disliked, found boring, or lacking in meaning. Take no more than five (5) minutes to make your list.

The spiritual journey is the soul's life commingling with ordinary life.
– Christina Baldwin

I long to accomplish a great and noble task, but it is my duty to accomplish humble tasks as though they were great and noble.
– Helen Keller

Enjoyable Domestic Activities	Unenjoyable Domestic Activities

Now that you've created a list, choose one domestic activity to explore. Time yourself, and limit your writing to no longer than fifteen (15) minutes. Write in your own stream-of-consciousness style. Don't concern yourself with grammar, punctuation, or spelling.

Your purpose is to learn about *your* domestic preferences, passions, gifts, and talents. You may realize that a domestic activity that you took for granted or thought meaningless has a special value for you. You may clarify the foundation of an important feeling or reclaim a quality from the past that defines your values in the present.

Allow yourself the freedom to shift through time. Explore periods of your life. Permit yourself to remember or imagine the past and muse about the future.

Natalie Goldberg, a well known teacher of writing, emphasizes that "writing is a physical act." Tell your own personal midrash, your own sacred, everyday stories. Trust that whatever you write will be useful to you. It may bring you closer to your authentic self. You may be surprised by a new perspective or meaning from your domestic life and about your worth as a woman.

Be sure to date your writing. After you've written, reflect on your experience and its meaning by writing Process Notes.

Have fun! And enjoy the gifts from the women in your virtual circle who have generously shared their insights as they explored ways they experienced the sanctity of hearth and home.

Every act, from planting a tree to recycling . . . can make a difference.
– Denise Linn

My second favorite household chore is ironing. My first being hitting my head on the top bunk bed until I faint.
– Erma Bombeck

The revolutions of the spinning wheel and the thwack of the loom sustained the rugged virtues of hard work, neighborliness, and unaffected piety.
– Laurel Thatcher Ulrich

Musing on My Domesticity

Process Notes

Cleaning Cupboards
by Laurie White

Once again I open the cupboard and the Tupperware falls on my toes. It's Mother's Day. I shouldn't have to clean! I should be pampered. I hate messy cupboards. I hate clutter. I hate unorganized chaos. I made the choice to pamper myself. I threw myself into the job of cleaning my cupboard. The cupboard consists of a large storage area on the bottom.

First thing to do is pull everything out. Oh, how satisfying it sounds to carelessly throw all the Tupperware on the floor. It reminds me of when the kids were toddlers and this cupboard was one of their favorite play places. Lindsey would crawl into the bottom and bang covers together. What a great Mother's day memory.

Next, clean off the shelves. As I wash them, I say to myself, "Boy, these were pretty clean." As I replaced and organized the Tupperware, I was trying to find a new and creative arrangement – maybe this new way would stay clean and organized.

"Ha! What a dream," I thought to myself.

Aaron entered the kitchen. "What are you doing? Cleaning cupboards?" He started to sort through the water bottles. How does one family accumulate 30 plus bottles? "Remember when we rode bikes at the cabin and we used these water bottles? Remember when I won this bottle at camp?" said Aaron. "Your dad and I bought these bottles when we were first married. They leak now but I've still held onto them," I said. Time to throw out old, time to move on.

With the cupboard clean, I stepped back, blurred my focus and took a big breath. The doors shut snugly. I opened and shut them several times. How beautiful to see everything organized. I wondered, "How long will this last?" Then a little voice in my head said, "Someday they'll all be moved on and your cupboards will be too clean, too organized, too perfectly kept. You won't have anyone around messing everything up looking for the right water bottle."

So I look forward to watching my cupboard get slowly messy, disorganized, chaotic. For then, I'll be able to put it all back together again. Being the mom, enjoying Mother's Day.

Take Time
by Sue Lewis

Softly, softly your hands caress me . . . slowly . . . patiently . . . gently in thoughtful motion.

Cool blue mists hover momentarily in the air and then tenderly connect on my cool surface.

Your absorbent cotton connects in concentric movements from general to specific,
moving in a spiral from outward to inward.

I feel the pressure of your hand and then the pause, repeated pressure and pause.

The light from the east dances across our space spotlighting this memorable moment.

This is not an ordinary experience; it is heightened with awareness.

So often this act had been done without consciousness.

Often in the past mediocrity defined the speed of delivery, not planned excellence.

But this time the sensuousness is so satisfying, the attention so welcome, all so right.

The ritual, as a messenger of magic, speaks its sensibility:

The stories are in the mundane. Take time to listen and prod.
And recognize in listening that time is not a god.
Doing it with mindful love brings incredible pleasure.
The consciousness of the moment is truly the measure.

I wish I could broadcast this far and wide,
But, alas, I am just the voice of a kitchen counter
who now shines with incredible pride!

A Daily Ritual
by Ethelyn Cohen

Know that the same woman
Who looks to bring meaning
Into an otherwise meaningless world
Gathers her thoughts and centers herself
Through the art of feather dusting.

It matters little the time of day
So long as she is focused
On such a solely simple task
Asking only that she be present.

Truth can be found here
There is no where else to seek it.
This clearly pure and simple act
Is one that only seldom fails
To clear away the dust.

Laundry I

by Mary Meinert

I feel accomplished and capable when my laundry is clean and folded in ready stacks. To have piles of dirty laundry about makes me weary. It's distracting and annoying. There's something very satisfying about putting away clean laundry. There – I am ready. Good to go.

Growing up as one of nine kids – no washer and dryer – we spent hours at the laundromat on Saturdays. If one needed something clean before "laundry day" – good luck! To this day grape soda reminds me of laundromats and soap.

Bleach and soap – let me at it! I love bleach with its promised whiteness. Many colored items I have ruined with my zealous bleaching techniques. And of course there is the 'bleach restriction' I suffered because of frustrated family. Oh well.

Laundry gives me a sense of order in the chaos. It is one place I can keep some order.

Laundry II

by Barbara J. Levie

I know windows are very distasteful – but the most pleasant thing I do around the house is laundry. Why? What is it I like when the machines basically do everything from start to finish, and all I have to do is fill and empty?

Each day the loads pile up like leaves after a voluptuous wind storm in the fall. Amazing that for only a few hours, there's nothing to wash and then – the pile begins again. . . . What I always find soothing is the ritual of pouring the powder into the stream of hot water. The flow of the water soothes and in the winter the steam pleases my dry skin. . . .

To load a washer is to fill and empty in a matter of moments. The same for the dryer. Laundry is fast and cleansing. Of all the things I do to maintain my home, laundry leaves me with a sense of cleanliness and energy. These two machines work so hard without me having to polish, dust, scrape, dry, replace, vacuum, flush – they simply do their work with grace and efficiency. P.S. Except for the lint trap

Ironing

by Lisa Gunther

I like to iron. I used to have an old wooden ironing board. Opening it up and setting it up and hearing its creaks and groans and smelling the smells of the pad and the cover felt good and right. Ironing always makes me hear the voices of the past – "Iron the collar and sleeves first; you'll wrinkle the body if you iron it first."

And the smell of the steam and bringing smoothness to the wrinkled clothes is satisfying. I love to iron while watching sports on television – both are boring activities that together create a perfect stretch of time. Nothing changes very quickly in either activity but at the end, each is complete.

I can see people from my past talking to us when we were kids. "Did she really iron sheets?" Yes, she did! And if they'd been hung outside, the outdoor and the iron smells merged, bringing a clean and ordered smell. It came with wisdom, advice, and the thumping of the iron.

I have had several irons over the years – looking for the one that felt right – heavy and solid – and made the right kind of hissing, steamy noise. I have – but don't use – the plate that you can put on the board to be sure that you don't burn the board cover. It's something you need to have.

Ironing can be a meditative experience – it's quiet and peaceful – not much movement. I hate to start the process, but once I start, I love to continue, ironing everything in sight. Bringing order to masses of wrinkles.

Mud Pies
by Vicki Pearson

Ceremoniously, like a master chef, I make mud-pies: carefully place them into discarded muffin tins and pie plates or roll and press them like fancy holiday cookies. I artfully decorate them with pebbles and twigs, then, wait for them to bake in hot summer sun.

Under a favorite shady willow tree, I set my child's table with a cherished tea set. On a serving plate, garnished with greens and berries from Mom's garden, the mud-pies are proudly served to playmates or dolls or patient kittens and puppies, bibs around their necks and ribbons tied to ears and tails. Sometimes, even Mom becomes a special guest.

Years later, the woman I've become receives a birthday greeting from a friend whose talents I admire. She quotes:
"All the genuine, deep delight of life is in showing
people the mud-pies you have made; and life is at
its best when we confidingly recommend our mud-
pies to each others' sympathetic consideration."

Then she adds:
"Oh, the joy of sharing mud-pies."

Does she know how completely I understand?
Is it folly to wish again for childhood . . . to want to capture life again that way?
Or is it in the shared understanding that we can live in both times at once?

Cooking
by Joan Munzner

My mother was an excellent cook and she also loved to eat. She had grown up in a poor family on a farm and while there was enough food for all ten, there were no frills or second helpings. It was a joy for her to be able to feed her family in a generous and lavish way. Growing up, I too loved to eat the food she prepared. She was particularly famous for her homemade bread, cinnamon rolls, pies, and cakes. We always had a garden which provided fresh vegetables complimented by a strawberry and raspberry patch which made for glorious summer breakfasts of freshly picked berries. My family was quite scornful of store-bought products and pitied our friends who were not so blessed with such culinary delights.

I did not help with preparing food. My sister and I set the table and helped with the dishwashing. Early on I considered myself an intellectual and felt that learning to cook was not something I would ever need to know. This all changed the first summer of being married. I did not work for the first time in many years and found I had time to read and cook.

I plunged into the domestic scene with great vigor, preparing two large meals every day (lunch and dinner). My cooking education began with at least one phone call to my mother per meal: how do you bake potatoes? How long does it take to roast a chicken? How do you roll out pie dough in a perfect circle? For my birthday at the end of that summer I received a *Betty Crocker Cookbook*. I learned the basics and eventually I graduated to Julia Child and was able to whip up a quiche Lorraine at the drop of a whisk. I still count cooking and reading among the pleasures of my life.

Cooking: Thanksgiving 2004
by Janet Kenney

The bookmark is already at the page in my *Joy of Cooking* cookbook, where I turn every year to read the instructions for preparing a turkey.

This year, the last year that I'll be doing this, as I have sworn to my middle-aged children, I see things in the instructions I never noticed before or ignored: instructions to wrap a string criss-cross fashion to the skewers. I skipped over that part as I have skipped over so much in my life, ignoring what I consider inconsequential.

The book is spotted with past years' cookings, the covers and part of the index are missing. What will I do with this book when I no longer host Thanksgiving? It makes me cry to think of throwing it away, like throwing away my life in small acts of disregard.

On the radio here in my room, "Make Our Garden Grow" by Leonard Bernstein, the final chorus from his musical *Candide,* and then a poem excerpt by Billy Collins. I think of the letter I still have from Leonard B. written to my father and feel even more connected to his music. No letter from Billy Collins, just two of his books, books unstained by Thanksgiving preparations, but read and listened to this day of days.

My Desk
by Jane L. Toleno

One of my favorite domestic places is my desk. It is simple and my husband Tom made it for me. My desk is located in our study which is near our kitchen – just right – I'm available when/if needed but blessedly removed. My desk is wide and deep enough to hold my favorite lamp and telephone, my computer keyboard and monitor, the printer and speakers, the scanner, my Braille writer and tape recorder.

I am short so the desk top is low. My hands rest on the computer keyboard easily. My pointer fingers confidently, competently find the identifying small dots on the F and J keys of this regular keyboard. My ears shut out household sounds. Tune in to the screen reader's voice that will come through the speakers once I start typing. It speaks whatever I type.

I am immediately at home when I come here. I am ready to feel, think, let the rest of my life drift into the background – wait for me! Here, I find out what is important. This desk is my hearth and altar.

I take my hands away from the keys, reach left and touch the lamp beside me. It has a shell as a lamp shade over the lit and heated bulb. My hands take turns. One hand, then the other hand; sometimes both hands move close to take in the warmth of the light; I imagine the light of the warmth.

I realize that I'm not quite settled yet. My left hand reaches up to the front of the first shelf above my computer desk. I keep treasures in front of all of the books I've read in one format or another. I move to touch the treasures now. One hand reaches, finds the chime and taps it with the small mallet. I breathe deep while the sound resonates inside and outside me. I ring it again and it calls forth my mind, heart, and spirit.

I pick up the talking feather my daughter Joanna gave me. I hold it and remember to let all parts of my being breathe, speak, remember, suggest next steps and dream; I agree anew to pass the feather from one to the next, to all; to hear them out before moving on.

My hand reverently touches the piece of obsidian stone – dark stone; translucent by feel and sight so lights shine within. Aren't we all capable of dark and lights?

Then I reach for the last treasure in the row, an emblem of bounty; the emblem of my Mother. It is a beautifully shaped, weighted apple. I smooth its cool brushed-satin texture against my cheek. I recall the star-shaped seed pattern in all apples. Such regenerative powers.

Domestic? We tend to think that domestic is primarily about tasks for, and care of others. I say that the heart of domesticity is This time and place – my desk. However limited, the time I spend here restores and generates enthusiasm within me.

I track down information. I ask my "I wonder if" questions. I keep records and I keep in touch with others who matter to me. I take deep breaths before I go to mop the floors in anticipation of grand babies arriving. Mopped floors keep the crawlers safe from harmful stuff loaded into indiscriminate mouths. I close my computer files as the doorbell rings.

I am so thankful that my computer talks. Since learning to use a computer, I have learned to write. Writing is hardly the first batch of words that pours from my heart and mouth. Writing is what happens after that. Writing is the saving of words and the returning to them later. It is the thought that I give them while I'm away and when I return to them. Writing is revising them and pulling out what might not need to be there – what must not be. Writing gives me the courage to clean out my own heart, mind, and spirit. Writing gives me delight in laughing. I take myself more and less seriously after writing.

What happens under my desk matters as much to me as what happens on the desktop or around it. Gala, dog guide number five, curls up near enough to me to touch me, and sometimes presses her head against my foot. She waits for me to finish. She knows that when she hears the "shut down" music it's time to pop up and DOOOOOO SOMETHING! What a girl.

Journey mercies to you all. Blessings be as, together, we help one another find places and times for our full selves in the busy lives we lead.

What did they do, our grandmothers, as they sat spinning all the day?
Are we not ourselves the web they wove?
– *Anonymous toast, Daughters of the American Revolution*

Home is where my dignity is.
– *Irshad Manji*

You need only claim the events of your life to make yourself yours.
– *Florida Scott-Maxwell*

We began this chapter with an introduction to Hestia, the Greek goddess of hearth and home. She represented the domestic arts, nurturance, protection, beauty, and spiritual light. When she was excluded and forgotten, so was what she stood for. Her loss was ours as well. We explored the rich meaning and power of the domestic dimension of our feminine nature to recover its value, and re-include this aspect of the divine within us.

You may still be asking, "How can Dina, or Hestia, or my housekeeping help me to create my legacy?" Knowing your history, reclaiming the legacies left you by your foremothers, and re-owning devalued feminine aspects of yourself, you become more of yourself and experience yourself as multi-dimensional, perhaps as more whole.

You have neither to hide nor silence parts of yourself. You have an authentic self, a structure created from a mixture of your unique past and present. This is the foundation for clarifying your values and exercising your voice. You are ready to create and document your legacies for the generations to come.

In chapters 3 and 4, we'll create elements to include in our spiritual-ethical wills. Congratulations on successfully concluding the preliminary work. Determining and expressing what matters is the stuff that legacy documents are made of. From here on, we'll experience ourselves as the link connecting the past and the future.

*May you experience
the abundant blessings
in your life, and the
joy of blessing others*

CHAPTER THREE

$\mathscr{B}$reaking the Silence

Transforming Our Wisdom into Blessings

Discovering Blessings

The ancient tradition of passing on values by instruction and blessing is the first element of the ethical will we'll explore. We find the prototype in Genesis. When Dina's father Jacob lay dying, he gathered his twelve sons, instructed and blessed them, and obtained their promise to bury him in Canaan with his ancestors.

Centuries later the Talmud clarified the responsibilities that fathers had to teach their sons: to study Torah, to learn a trade, and to learn to swim. We can understand those obligations metaphorically as preparing the next generation for survival in the physical world, in the world of relationships, and in the ethical-moral-spiritual realm. You may notice similarities in the instructions you received from your own family: be good, work hard, and take care of yourself and your family.

Learning about the tradition of men writing ethical wills made me want to write for my children and loved ones. I wasn't about to be excluded because I am a woman. When I heard Joan Drury, contemporary author and philanthropist, express her inspirational belief that "women's written words would change the world," I vowed to create a resource that would make the ethical will a tool friendly to contemporary women of all backgrounds, faiths, and circumstances, so we could build a new tradition: documenting our legacies.

I changed the name from ethical will to differentiate it from the patriarchal tradition, and to emphasize its spiritual nature. I call it "the spiritual-ethical will." I believe that writing our legacies is a spiritual endeavor linking us to past and future generations.

Nowhere in the archetypal myths of Western culture could I find a feminine voice documenting her legacy, someone whose words could be a template for women of the twenty-first century. But I did find a model in the writings of a seventeenth century German Jewish widow, mother of fourteen. And she couldn't have been more perfect.

In the year 1690, Glückel began writing a diary. Translated and published in the twentieth century, its title is *The Memoirs of Glückel of Hameln*. Had I been its translator, I would have called this remarkable document *The Spiritual-Ethical Will of Glückel of Hameln*. Anne Roiphe wrote about the relevancy of Glückel's writing in her 1981 book, *Generation without Memory*:

"What caused her to write at all? She was alone and among the very first. She claims that she is telling her children the history of their family so that they will know where they come from and who their people were. But I expect that's only an excuse, a rational face on the less explicable impulse to let one's life stand as an example, to give it some sense and some order, to take some perspective and make peace with the chaos within. . . .

"Glückel was among the first writers in the Western world to notice that babies and dowries, relations of in-laws and the rise and fall of individual bank accounts were in fact subjects for the written page – subjects for the next generation to wonder over. Her act of writing, an act so isolated . . . is an act so daring, a compulsion so pure, that one can only marvel. . . .

"Glückel was forty-four when she began to write. . . . I include this . . . to suggest that mid-forties is obviously a time when women begin to feel the urgency to make sense of their lives, connect themselves and their children to family history, and to leave a legacy."

Here, excerpted, but in Glückel's own voice, are three instructions she wrote to her sons: (I chose these of many in this 277 page memoir to correlate with the ethical will tradition as defined in the Talmud.)

- Diligently go about your business, providing your wife and children a decent livelihood
- Know from what sort of people you have sprung
- During the time for prayers, do not stand about and talk of other things

Become daring enough to demand your rights.
– Emma Goldman

The world is waiting for us to bless it.
– Naomi Levy

Harvesting the Legacies from Our Foremothers

Like Glückel, our mothers and foremothers had aspirations and hopes for us. Some of what they passed on was stated clearly in words, but often we were instructed by their behavior, which modeled what was appropriate to the times, the family's tradition, or the ways religion and faith were lived and practiced.

We may be unsure even now how we received those implicit instructions. Maybe we ate or drank the message; perhaps we were swaddled in the hope or dream. It's possible that we received our foremothers' legacies by osmosis, from the hereditary ethos of being women.

Not all legacies we received were useful or helpful to us. Some of what was passed on to us may have been unrealistic, impractical, even abusive. Perhaps injunctions echoed from the deep well of generations of family secrets. Maybe they were misunderstandings or distortions of ethical or moral truths, twisted by circumstance and experience.

Planning the future without knowing the past is like planting cut flowers.
– Maureen Dowd

Each turn in a life defines,
but movement without clarity
means nothing.
– Carol Edgarian

Use the following template to document legacies you received from your mother and foremothers. Write a positive and a negative legacy in each of the three categories. The first is for legacies about the physical-material world; include legacies about care of your body, health, and the world of work. The second is for legacies about ethics and relationships with others; include parents, children, extended family, men, friends, people similar to and different from you. The third is for legacies you received about moral values, faith and religion, the spiritual realm.

Time yourself, and limit your writing to no longer than ten (10) minutes. Be sure to date your writing. Here are examples shared by women from your virtual legacy circle:

#1   *Positive:* Take good care of your body; it is the sacred vessel
       that carries your soul in the world.
       Negative: Gardening and cooking are things for other people
       to be good at.

In search of my mother's
garden, I found my own.
– Alice Walker

#2   *Positive:* Value your women friends.
       Negative: Being a mother is a totally fulfilling and absorbing
       role for a woman.

#3   *Positive:* Respect and take responsibility for the environment;
       nature is wondrous, spiritual, and full of beauty.
       Negative: Church, ministers, and God don't provide
       much help.

Legacies from My Foremothers

Date of writing:

#1 (THE PHYSICAL-MATERIAL WORLD)

Positive:

Negative:

#2 (RELATIONSHIPS)

Positive:

Negative:

#3 (THE ETHICAL-MORAL-SPIRITUAL REALM)

Positive:

Negative:

Discovering Your Values and Wisdom

Every mother contains her daughter in herself and every daughter her mother, and every woman extends backward into her mother and forward into her daughter.
– Carl Jung

We are now creating the future by the formation of the present.
– Myles Horton
& Paulo Freire

Having gathered legacies we received from the past, we turn now to our lives. Each of us has a unique life story, our own experiences and perspectives. The values and meaning we have culled from living our lives are a source of the wisdom we can pass on to those we love. You may find your instructions similar to or very different from the legacies of instruction that you received from your foremothers.

Consider your passions and values; take into account your experiences and life lessons learned. Write one instruction to fit each of the three categories: physical-material, ethics-relationships, and moral-spiritual. Limit your reflection and writing to ten (10) minutes. Be sure to date your instruction.

Don't be concerned about the form your writing takes. Your instruction may be just a phrase or a sentence or two. What matters now is to define your values and clarify what's significant to you.

My Instructions for Future Generations

Date of writing:

INSTRUCTION #1 (ABOUT THE PHYSICAL-MATERIAL WORLD)

_____

_____

_____

_____

_____

INSTRUCTION #2 (ABOUT RELATIONSHIPS)

_____

_____

_____

_____

_____

INSTRUCTION #3 (ABOUT THE ETHICAL-MORAL-SPIRITUAL REALM)

_____

_____

_____

_____

_____

Transforming Instructions into Blessings

Being able to receive a legacy may depend on the words and tone of the message. We're all familiar with being instructed. Even when well-meaning, instructions can be received as commands, demands, even punishment. Their tone may seem harsh, unfeeling, or cold. You may wonder whether the instruction is more about the person giving it than a gift of love to be received by you.

When I was writing *Women's Lives, Women's Legacies,* it became clear that instructions came from the "head" and that our legacy writing was about giving gifts from our "hearts." Perhaps somewhat exaggerated and stereotypical, I began to think about instructions as masculine. I was committed to finding ways that we could express our ideas and feelings in a style and with words that honored our feminine essence. Transforming instructions into blessings became central to writing a spiritual-ethical will. Women's legacies need to be expressed in a womanly way. Our legacies need to be blessing-full.

Marc Gafni, author of *Soul Prints,* explains: "Blessing in biblical myth is more than the transmission of good wishes or spiritual protection. . . . Each child is granted his own blessing, reflecting his unique destiny."

Before you try your hand at transforming one of the instructions you've written into a blessing, let's look again at Glückel's seventeenth century words of instruction. Try to experience how her thoughts might have been received differently written as blessings:

#1 *Glückel's instruction about the physical-material world:*
    Diligently go about your business, providing your wife and
    children a decent livelihood.
    As a blessing: May you find joy in your chosen work, and may
    that work provide a decent livelihood for you and your family.

#2   *Glückel's history instruction:* Know from what sort of people you have sprung.

        As a blessing: May you cherish your family history as it sustains you in a matrix (womb) of love and tradition.

#3   *Glückel's ethical-moral-spiritual instruction:* During the time for prayers, do not stand about and talk of other things.

        As a blessing: May God's spirit fill you and help you focus your prayers.

Most of us assume that blessings are supposed to be delivered in houses of worship by the clergy. Like other intimate aspects of our culture, blessings have been turned over to professionals; yet in the Bible, not only does God bless humanity, but fathers and leaders bless their sons and the people. Women need to reclaim this powerful tradition to include in our legacies.

Getting started may be the most difficult part of rewriting your instruction. Most of us do not yet naturally think or write in blessing form. Did you notice that each of Glückel's instructions that I rewrote as blessings began with the word "may"? Here are some phrases you might want to try out to see how they work for you:

- May you always . . .
- May God (or your Higher Power) bless you with . . .
- May you be blessed as I have been with . . .
- I bless you with . . .
- I wish you . . .
- I hope for you . . .

Choose one of your three instructions and write it below as a blessing. Write your instruction first, and then in no longer than five (5) minutes, experiment with writing that instruction in the form of a blessing.

To give someone a blessing is the most significant affirmation we can offer. . . . A blessing touches the original goodness of the other and calls forth his or her Belovedness.

– Henri Nouwen

We can fail to appreciate our innate power to bless if we regard blessing as a force so awesome and special, it must lie beyond our ordinary capabilities. Then there is the danger of losing its humanity and capacity to connect with us in our everyday lives.

– David Spangler

Writing My Instruction as a Blessing   Date of writing:

MY INSTRUCTION:

_____

_____

_____

_____

_____

_____

WRITTEN AS A BLESSING:

_____

_____

_____

_____

_____

_____

_____

Set your blessing aside for a short time or overnight. Return to edit it if you want to make changes before you share it. Before you begin any rewriting, consider some of the following:

- Reread your blessing aloud to yourself.
- Have your words adequately and clearly conveyed the message you mean to send? You may need to seek help from a thesaurus or distill your blessing so your recipient is not distracted from the blessing's essentials.
- Have you really written a blessing or just rewritten a command or demand, camouflaging it by beginning with the word "may"? I know I can feel the difference because the pressure awakens my teenage rebel who wants no intrusion from my elders.
- Have you used words that don't seem quite right or words that don't sound like you? The last thing you want is for someone fifty or a hundred years from now to discard the blessing because it sounds like it came from a book. You want the gift of blessing to also give the reader a sense of who you were and what your values were.
- What is the tone of your blessing? Anger and resentments belong in private journals. I use the Buddhist tenet: "Do no harm" to test my blessings. Though we can't control how our blessings will be understood, we can control what we write. Imagine someone reading your blessing fifty years from today: What tone do you want emanating from your words?
- Imagine yourself as the recipient of the blessing: how do you respond to it? Does your heart open or slam shut?

Limit your editing of this first draft to five (5) minutes. If you're not finished after five minutes, continue to edit, referring to the questions above as a guide. Work through several drafts, until you are satisfied.

What you don't transform, you will transmit.
– Richard Rohr

When we bless, we are working with God.
– Joseph Edelheit

Editing My Blessing

Date of writing:

Processing

When you are finished, reflect on your experience writing a blessing. Blessings feel just right to many women: written from their hearts, gentle, and intimate. Other women distrust blessings; they find them indirect, manipulative, a style used to control others. Writing Process Notes is a method to use your intuition to check in with your sense of truth. Discover the style that, though perhaps new and unfamiliar, is exactly the approach that fits for you as you document your legacies. If you are moved by the spiritual power and integrity of blessings as I am, you may use them frequently as you write your spiritual-ethical will.

Your process writing may clarify more than the style of writing that fits for you; it may suggest the kind of content that you want to include in your legacy. Here are some suggestions to guide your reflection:

- Observe ways in which the legacies you received were instructive (helped you to understand your life and your history), but are not the blessings you want to pass on to the next generation.
- Consider the practicality of separating legacies/blessings into the material, relationship, and spiritual levels of your life. [For example, a woman friend confided that she was often awakened from sound sleep blessed with insights. She shared one: a sign that might have advertised a diner, that kept flashing E-A-T. Checking her stomach and not feeling the least bit hungry at three in the morning, she was bewildered. The virtual neon continued to flash until she realized her lack of self-care during a period of stress. The sign was about feeding her emotional and spiritual needs, not her stomach.]
- Although we are working with one blessing here, be aware that you started with three instructions, and probably have many more to work with at your leisure. (Note: For those

With each blessing uttered we extend the boundaries of the sacred and ritualize our love of life.
— Lawrence Kushner

I want to leave something behind, and what a blessing it is to know I can.
— Rosanne Barr,
  The Actors Studio,
  9/9/01

A blessing is a true gift, and not a transaction in disguise; it's freeing…
It does not obligate either one.
— David Spangler

Women will change the nature of power rather than power changing the nature of women.
— Bella Abzug

May you be a blessing to this world, and many blessings surround you now and always.
— Naomi Levy

interested in additional reflections and writing about women's instructions and blessings, see chapter 8 "Sharing Your Values and Blessings," in *Women's Lives, Women's Legacies.* Two books written in the 1990s may also interest you: *The Measure of our Success: A Letter to My Children and Yours,* by Marion Wright Edelman, founder of the national organization, The Children's Defense Fund, and *Everything I Know: Basic Rules from a Jewish Mother,* Sharon Strassfeld's gift to her daughter who was leaving home for college.)

• Consider the significance of an instruction and a blessing. Notice the different kind of power each holds. Are there situations in which an instruction may be more appropriate? Are there circumstances in which a blessing is preferable?

Process Notes

Sharing Yourself as Part of Your Blessing

When we write our spiritual-ethical wills, we have the opportunity to be known, seen, and valued by those we love. We do this by telling those we love who we are. You can add a sliver of who you are as you complete your blessing, at the same time clarifying why this particular blessing is significant coming from you.

Perhaps it's easier to hide behind a lecture of instructions, or the distance that becoming a "blessor" provides. But including personal material, although it makes us vulnerable, is far more effective than sermonizing. Future generations will appreciate knowing the real you – and they'll be more likely to accept your wisdom when they understand the source of your gift.

As a gift to your Virtual Legacy Circle, Laura Hansen, a legacy writer and independent bookstore owner, shared her process of transforming an instruction into a blessing including her personal understanding.

Instruction: Be generous and open-hearted as your grandfather always was, helping others often and quietly.

Blessing (before editing): May you find that you are guided through life by generosity rather than avarice. May you always remember your grandfather and how he gave of his time and possessions to help others without asking for repayment or acknowledgment.

Blessing (after editing and including a personal insight): May you always be guided through life by generosity as your grandfather was. I was never able to give as easily as he. I've always held everything too tightly.

To launch her daughter who was leaving for college, Sharon Strassfeld wrote her a legacy book. Here is one of her instructions. "When you walk along the street, look into people's faces as you pass them." Then Strassfeld added how she viewed her daughter and shared her own experience.

Words must not fall off our lips like dead leaves in the autumn. They must rise like birds out of the heart and into the vast expanse of eternity.
– Abraham Joshua Heschel

Blessings exist for the magnificent and the mundane.
– Lawrence A. Hoffman

"Kayla, you taught me this when you began your own personal home-lessness project as a [high school] student. . . . You would use your allowance to buy food and drinks, which you distributed to the homeless on your walk up to school at 122nd Street.

"I was awed, as I have often been, by the purity of your soul, and you taught me to extend my rule about looking at people as I pass them on the street even to those whom, in our society, have no faces."

Being inspired by Strassfeld, I wrote to my own children: "May you be blessed with compassionate and wise eyes: eyes that see beyond the face of cir-cumstance, that see the spark of the Divine deep within you and everyone on our planet. I learned about this while I sat reading on a subway in Manhattan. A pregnant, homeless woman entered the car, and began to beg. I averted my eyes, buried my face in my book, and clasped my heart and my purse tightly. Silent minutes passed and suddenly the woman began to shout at the riders – crying out that it was okay if we didn't give her money, but it wasn't okay to avoid looking her in the face – that she was a human being! She picked up her bags and lurched through the door into the next train car.

"I was shocked and shamed. Since then, even if I choose not to give to a person begging, I look the person in the eye. I feel more human when I acknowledge another's humanity." (See the Appendix for a newer version of this letter, written in accordance with a legacy letter template. pp. 126-128)

I define instructions as mental, coming from our heads, and blessings, coming from our hearts. This last addition to your edited blessing adds your soul.

Copy your edited blessing in the space provided. Before you begin to write, take time to reflect on why this blessing is important to you: When and what did you experience or learn that makes this blessing personally significant? What is the emotion, struggle, belief, or secret that is related to this blessing? What do you want to share about yourself that will help the

Blessings give reverent and routine voice to our conviction that life is good, even and especially when life is cold and dark. Indeed to offer blessings at such times may be our only deliverance.
– Lawrence Kushner

We bless ourselves as we bless one another.
– John Morton

And there are those who have little and give it all. These are the believers in life and the bounty of life, and their coffer is never empty.
– Kahlil Gibran

recipient receive both you and your blessing? When you're ready, write *you* into the blessing. Take no longer than five (5) minutes to imbue your blessing with your core self. When you have finished, read it to yourself, and edit it until you are satisfied that you have integrated yourself into your blessing. Then be inspired by the soul-full blessings shared by women in your virtual legacy circle.

Adding Me to My Edited Blessing

Date of writing:

MY EDITED BLESSING:

_____

_____

_____

_____

_____

_____

_____

ADDING ME TO MY EDITED BLESSING:

_____

_____

_____

_____

_____

_____

_____

"Loss," a short story by Susan Tilsch, records a dying mother talking to her son. As she speaks, she blesses him. The reader is moved to connect deeply with the character of the mother as she shares her vulnerability, her authentic self, her soul. Here is an excerpt (from *Women's Lives, Women's Legacies,* pages 232–234).

The wisdom kept pouring out. He couldn't help wondering if she had written out some of her words beforehand. "May there come a time when the critical voice that is inside all of us can be quiet inside you." He could see her feeling the need to explain more. "It has been my life's struggle to accept myself as I am, that I am not as good and as perfect as I would like to be. My critical voices have brought me a lot of pain, getting in the way of my living joyfully and fully." He could feel a deep integrity in her words. Her voice lightened as she continued. "It helped when I came to see my own special gifts, my own uniqueness. I see imperfections more as humanness now."

She paused again, starting a new direction.

"Listening is one of the greatest gifts to give to others and yourself. When I have been truly listened to, it has allowed me to feel loved and valued. It is hard to be a good listener. When I have listened to others, I am startled at how much I hear and how much more people will say." She hoped he was listening and taking it all in.

It seemed as if she could go on forever, but suddenly she stopped. There was silence, leaving again only the sound of shallow breathing. For a moment he feared it was over. Then some words again. "Walking on the beach . . . those pelicans . . . the seagulls." She twisted slightly in bed. "Big white snowflakes . . . deer tracks." She seemed to be moving through the seasons. "Those yellow warblers in the spring . . ." she trailed off. More silence. And then he knew it was over. She had finished.

INSTRUCTION: Believe in yourself.
BLESSING: May you always be blessed with a deep belief in yourself, a knowing and acceptance of your inner wisdom, your God-given talents and uniqueness, and your innate value as a wonderful, lovable human being. This is something I didn't believe about myself for most of my life and it was a very painful way to live.

INSTRUCTION: Trust in yourself – be content with yourself.
BLESSING: May you always be happy with who you are – because you are the Best. I never felt that I was good enough, that I had done well enough, that I had tried hard enough. I felt that I should have done/been more than I was. I would have you know that you are and always have been more than good enough.

INSTRUCTION: Don't give yourself away – Practice self love.
BLESSING: I spent so many years giving what I didn't have: peace of mind, self worth, wholeness. May you see how much you are loved and honored and valued simply by being yourself.

FOR A GRANDSON:
BLESSING: *May you always jump for joy at the sight of a snowstorm. May you always scream with excitement at the sound of the words 'Dairy Queen'. May you always forget to go on the swings and slide at the park and simply revel at the feeling of making snow angels in the crushed rock.*
May you always know how much I love you and how much you've taught me about truly 'living in the moment'. Love, Grandpa

FOR A MARRIAGE:
BLESSING: *(Excerpt) May you continue to tell your stories of ancestors past and be inspired to create stories about your new life. May the Holy One of Blessing bless you and your marriage.*

FOR A NEW JOB:
BLESSING: *(Excerpt)* I knew that when you got up at your regular time the day after you were laid off to start your job search, we would be fine. Now as you start your new job and a new chapter in your career, may you begin with anticipation, excitement and confidence.

INSTRUCTION: Share your inner thoughts and feelings with another person.

BLESSING: My aloneness in life melted away as I opened my feelings to others. May you experience this opening up and this closeness with others.

PROCESS NOTES: As I think about the changes I made in the two versions, I feel that there is more depth and more softness in the second. Also, I am providing more free choice whether to receive or act on my blessing. It feels like my hope for another, not my forced will.

Most importantly, I feel that in the second version, I am passing on my experience. I am sharing a blessing which grew from what I have learned in the experience of my life. There is an empowering effect of having written the revised version. I am reminded of the strength and uniqueness of my own life. It is from this place that I have found what I wish to pass on as a blessing.

Jacob Blesses His Daughter, Dina

Before leaving chapter 3 and the subject of blessings, we return once more to Jacob of Genesis, the man whose blessings became the prototype for the traditional ethical will. Jacob's life ended as he blessed his sons, but from his youth we learn his own deep yearning to be blessed by his father. In *Soul Prints*, Marc Gafni explains, "Jacob, in an act of undeniable deception, had stolen from him [his older brother, Esau] the blessing of their father, Isaac – a blessing originally intended for Esau, the firstborn."

Gafni continues, "We all seek the blessings of the father, sometimes so desperately do we want it that we engage in deception in order to receive it." Moderately interesting, you might be thinking, but what does it matter to me, to my children or grandchildren?

I agree wholeheartedly with Gafni's theory. I believe that women of every generation yearn to be blessed by their fathers, and most of us have been disappointed. It becomes clear as we practice courage, discover our voices, and weave words to bless others, that we yearn to be blessed ourselves. Both blessing and receiving blessing are components of realizing the sacred text of our own lives.

As we earlier used the time-honored tradition of midrash to include ourselves in the stories and wisdom of sacred texts, so we do here. This time it's for the purpose of providing healing for the Dinas and Jacobs who lived in past generations and in our own.

Use your intuition and creativity to step back into time past. Imagine that you are Jacob. Become Jacob. Take five (5) minutes to write a blessing to your daughter, Dina. Note: There are two sections provided for you to write a second blessing if you choose.

Have you but one blessing, my father? Bless me, even me also. . . . And Esau lifted up his voice and wept.
– Genesis 27:38

A blessing is much like a transfusion or an act of resuscitation in which new blood and new breath – a new sense of presence and life – is given to us so that we may be empowered, restored, or revitalized.
– David Spangler

Sadness . . . not to have a father who could bless me with song, with the permission to be foolish.
– Naomi Shihab Nye

Jacob Blessing Dina

Date of writing:

Dear Dina,

Jacob

Date of writing:

Dear Dina,

Jacob

Processing

Reflect on your experience writing a blessing as Jacob, the father, to your daughter, Dina.

- Because we live in patriarchy as did Dina, most of us have not been blessed by our real fathers. Consider ways your life is and was affected by having been blessed or not by your father.

- Your Jacob may sound like your own idealized father. Further, you may have written a blessing as Jacob that resonates with the modern Dina who lives inside you. Imagining yourself as Jacob blessing Dina has the potential for deep healing. You may have become the Jacob you wished your own father to be, and that ideal father gave you the exact blessing for which you've yearned as long as you can remember.

- Consider which realms (material, relationships, spiritual) your Jacob blessing addressed, and see how that is useful information for you living your life today.

- Finally, enjoy and be nurtured by the examples of women like you and me who have contributed their Jacob-Dina blessings to our virtual circle.

Everything unborn in us and in the world needs blessing.
– Rachel Naomi Remen

A blessing is the passing of spirit between us.
– David Spangler

Process Notes

Jacob Blessing Dina

Dear Dina,

You sit at the base of my heart. Time and culture denied you the gifts and love I was afraid to give. . . . May you forgive me. . . . To honor that hidden love of father to daughter I send you this blessing . . . may you feel the quiet strength of a committed love. . . . May you know in every bone of your body that you are a precious beauty. . . . May my unspoken love now leap the valley of tradition and mightily celebrate you.

> *[Process Notes: Where does this come from? Don't need to know. . . . I savor just feeling it. And, somewhere within I know my own father now finds the courage to say these same things to me — I would also like to hear those words from my husband. So, I hold these words as if he could speak them. They are words I need to hear. I don't understand what fear holds some men back from sharing their heart and giving needed encouragement. But, blessed me. I have found ways to surround myself with women who are not afraid to be in their strength and hearts]*

Come close, dearest Dina, my precious and most prized daughter. As I take my leave of this world, let me whisper these words in your ear. . . . I bless you first with a forgiving spirit that would help to heal this tired old man's heart and soul. For all I never said, couldn't or wouldn't say, will you let me bless you now, and all the days of your life, with the knowledge and security that I loved you in the only way I knew how . . . you are my only Dina.

> *[Process Notes: Change one letter, and this could be ME with my own father.*
> *– Dona]*

My dearest daughter, May you be blessed as the mother of a tribe – the tribe of the injured and forgotten women. May this tribe hold you beloved and revered throughout the ages.

Bless you, my daughter. Though you may not have forgiven me, I bless you.

My dearest Dina, my only daughter, how I wish I could go back in time and make right all that has been done wrong to you. From the deepest part of my heart and soul I bless you in God's name and pray that your life is one that you will cherish.

I pray that God gives you better judgment than I and more courage to stand up for your convictions.

Daughter of my heart: may you live with pride, confidence and hope. Your God recognizes you even if men don't.

Dearest Dina, Blest are you like the moon among stars, the sun among planets, and hope among life's desperation.

My daughter Dina: I bless you with 1/13th of my property.

To my daughter whom I love as an eldest son: may you be blessed with all that is good. Produce your own voice and share it with your brothers to mend this family.

I, your father, bless you my child and daughter – blossom, believe, and love.

I want to bless you, my only daughter, so you may know that you are and have always been loved, to keep you safe and offer you wisdom. And accept my apology for the hurt I caused you.

My daughter Dina, may the hand of God touch all you do.

CHAPTER FOUR

$\mathscr{B}$reaking the Silence

Death through the Lens of Legacy

As we accept the blessings and the sacredness of our lives, then surely death, an integral part of life, must be sacred too. Women's spirituality is interwoven with the beginnings of life: carrying, bringing, nurturing, and protecting life. So too we embrace the end of life. Women are caregivers and comforters of the dying and the mourners.

Yet death and dying are taboo subjects. When we look back at Jacob of Genesis, we find no such secret or silence. After Jacob blessed his sons, he wrested a vow from them: bury him not in Egypt, but return his bones to the family's ancestral burial place in Canaan.

It should be as natural for us to address death in our legacy documents as it was in biblical times, but it's not. I searched historical literature and Western culture looking for a feminine voice to guide us, a woman who dared to break the silence, to speak the truths that others feared even to whisper. We needed a Dina, a Hestia, or a Glückel as a model. Investigating recent times, I found one, and she was just what the doctor ordered.

Poet Ruth F. Brin writes a stunning statement defining the difference between death in Jacob's time and now, and calls us to use our power to make a difference today and for future generations. The poem, "The Death of Jacob: Genesis 49" is from the 1999 edition of her book, *Harvest: Collected Poems and Prayers.*

As Jacob lay dying
he had the strength to bless his sons
and time to speak his prophecies.

But in our time
death is a hungry hunter
pursuing us on the highway,
overtaking us in the fastest planes;

Dying, there may be for us no long farewells,
no blessings, and no prophecies.

Living, then, we must bless our children,
placing our hands upon them
and turning their faces toward God;
living, we must struggle for a better day.

To foretell the future
may be a patriarch's privilege,
but to take the future in our hands is urgent
and to make it good shall be our human glory.

Oh God of Jacob, while yet we live,
help us to guide our children in love and wisdom,
help us now to build a world of peace.

In her internationally-renowned first book, *On Death and Dying,* Elisabeth Kübler-Ross, M.D., broke our society's taboo of silence about grief, death, and the dying process. *Time Magazine* named her one of the hundred greatest scientists and thinkers of the century. What was revolutionary in 1969 is commonly accepted today: that people who are dying are grieving and have lots to say about the process.

Using Kübler-Ross as our model is an apt memorial: a tribute to her life and her work. She died August 24, 2004. Although her well-known stages of dying may not accurately describe everyone's experience, her legacy was instrumental. She gave us a new perspective. She liberated our voices about accepting the normality of death as a part of life.

Today, thanks to Kübler-Ross, it is normal and natural to consider our own deaths, and to communicate to our loved ones about this reality. One day we will no longer be on earth with them in the form we have today. Marrying the ethical will of biblical tradition with the medical work of a courageous twentieth century woman gives us permission to reflect on and consider our own deaths, and how we want to be treated, memorialized, mourned, and remembered.

You may ask, "How does *my* death relate to my legacy?" It is in recognizing our mortality that we find life precious. Acknowledging death allows us to appreciate and live life more fully every day, with awe and gratitude for our blessings. Consider the significance of expressing this value as a part of your legacy. Here's an instruction: "Be grateful for your life; live every day as if it were your last!" Unpalatable? Likely to be misunderstood as pious or controlling? How about wording it then as a beautiful blessing? "May you experience and appreciate the abundance of your life; may you live every day to the fullest."

This legacy is even more effective if you express it by the way you live your life. Articulating your requests about having your life end with dignity

To live life fully, one must accept that it ends
– Irvin Yalom

There are times when we must search for the courage to embrace death instead of fighting it.
– Naomi Levy

How shall I live, knowing I will die?
– Wayne Muller

Life is a splendid torch which I have got hold of for the moment, and I want to make it burn as brightly as possible before handing it on to future generations.
– George Bernard Shaw

We've Woven You a Blanket
by Sue Renwick

We' woven you a blanket
   with strands made of many miles and many trips
We've woven you a blanket
   with airplane tickets, and rented cars, with families and jobs left behind
We've woven you a blanket
   with endless hours in waiting rooms, waiting with stomachs and
   shoulders tight
We've woven you a blanket
   with meals in cafeterias and cafes across the street
We've woven you a blanket
   with walks, with nights spent in beds not our own
We've woven you a blanket
   holding your hand, rubbing your feet
We've woven you a blanket
   kissing your forehead, arranging your hair
We've woven you a blanket
   with your readings and your favorite music
We've woven you a blanket
   with prayers and the help of friends

We've woven you a blanket
    moving aside the tubes and machinery that plot your life force
We've woven you a blanket
    with our hugs for each other – our tears – our laughter
We've woven you a blanket
    filled with gratitude for a life shared
    for forgiveness given and received
We've woven you a blanket
    with our willingness to make the decision about your living
    with our telling you we were okay
    giving you our permission to let go
We've woven you a blanket
    with our love for you and for each other
We've woven you a blanket
    wanting to keep you warm and safe
Some strands may be scratchy-imperfect
Some still to be done – but
We've woven you a blanket – as best we could.

and respect, demonstrates that you care enough about yourself to ask to be memorialized in ways real and personal and meaningful to you. It will teach by your living example that your loved ones have lives and deaths that are precious too. What better legacy can we leave future generations?

Sometimes acknowledging our mortality stimulates deep thinking, consideration of life purpose, and our need to have our lives make a difference. But most of us, living our busy lives, don't spend our days contemplating death or how we want to be remembered. Yet you know what you love about life and can use that knowledge to express what you find precious and beautiful. That defines you as uniquely as other values.

Document what you love about your life. Reflect on your values and what you value about your life. Write sentences that begin with either: "What I love about my life is . . ." or "What I will miss when I die. . . ."

Write only one thing in each sentence. Be specific. Write things that only you know about, things that you care deeply about, that will die with you if you don't record them. Consider and feel how these things make your life delicious and delightful.

Complete these sentences as many times as you can in the allotted time. Wander through all the aspects and components of your life. Consider your passions as well as your values. Take time to focus your attention on your senses: smelling, touching, hearing, seeing, tasting. For example, "I love the sound of a canoe paddle dipping into a calm lake."

Consider relationships, social, family, communal, and private moments that you value. Move gently from memory to meaning, from the present to the past, from home to the whole planet. For example, "I'll miss seeing my kids' and grandchildren's lives unfold."

Time yourself, and limit your writing to no longer than fifteen (15) minutes. Date your writing. After you've written, read Vicki Pearson's generous gift to your virtual legacy circle, her response to this exercise.

What's Precious about My Life and Death   Date of writing:

WHAT I LOVE ABOUT MY LIFE IS:

_____

_____

_____

_____

_____

_____

WHAT I'LL MISS WHEN I'M GONE:

_____

_____

_____

_____

_____

_____

What I'll Miss When I'm Gone: These Things I Love
By Vicki Pearson

I love the streets of London
and Bellagio and San Francisco,
the fjords of Norway,
the backroads of Vermont,
Arizona's Oak Creek Canyon,
the North Shore of Lake Superior,
the grand, Grand Canyon
and Porto Fino.

I love white sand beaches,
farmer's markets and art fairs,
coffee houses and flower shops,
book stores and art galleries . . .
and I love cabins in the woods.

I love long walks and good talks,
driving in the country,
cross-country skiing,
practicing yoga,
seeking sea shells and small smooth stones,
gazing into a blazing fire,
and knowing I have a great book to read.

I love kitchen conversation and good coffee,
park benches and jig-saw puzzles,
kaleidoscopes and family pictures,
notes and letters from long-lost friends,
Christmas trees full of ornaments and lights
and singing Christmas carols.

I love mornings' first light and sunsets,
a starry night a full moon in the velvet sky,
lightening and thunderstorms,
rain on the roof and sun on my back,
the splendor of autumn,
gentle snowfall, waving wheat fields,
soaring eagles, gold finch
and scarlet cardinals.

I love the sounds of waves of lapping at the shore,
fountains and waterfalls,
wind chimes and music boxes,
refrains of majestic choral music
and wind in pine trees.

I love the smell of fragrant spring blossoms,
the desert after rainfall,
cookies baking, clean sheets,
a beach fire in September
and lemons, freshly cut.

I love the taste of crisp, crunchy apples,
hot tea, warm oatmeal-raisin cookies,
almonds, pistachios, caramels and crème brulee,
spicy jellybeans, licorice and popcorn for dinner,
bright, red juicy strawberries
and kumquats.

I love the feel of creative juices flowing:
clay in my hands . . . from earth to vessel,
journals and notebooks and beautiful papers,
fine-tipped pens,
the hand of beautiful fabrics,
the blending of colors and textures.
I love the feel of a luxurious massage
and holding the hand of someone I love.

I love to wear cashmere sweaters and old jeans,
terry robes and satin jimmies,
warm socks and summer sandals,
soft, supple leather and pearl earrings.

I love all shades of white:
down quilts and pillows,
big, thirsty bath towels,
tile floors, lustrous wood
and white linen. . .
old sterling silver and crystal glassware,
candlelight anywhere . . . everywhere.
the silken white of the chambered nautilus,
fragrant springtime paper whites,
freshly cut stately white tulips, white lilies and daisies.

I love being asked for advice by my children . . .
and listened to and heard . . . if not heeded.
I love hearing my children being complimented
and paying compliments.

I love being Nana to my grandchildren;
cherishing their imagination and spirit.
I love giggles and freckles and belly laughs,
baby toes and baby fingers,
growing minds and bodies
and changing voices.

I love being a trusted friend,
I love a good discussion
and a heated debate.
I love knowing I have been understood.

I love being in my kitchen, in my garden
and in my bed.
I love a day without television or telephone
or telemarketers
and I love having time alone.

I love thinking people, thoughtful people,
compassionate people and wise people,
artists and their crafts, good teachers,
fine lectures and inspiring words . . .
ah, yes, I love words.

I love The Cape Ann, The Razor's Edge and Out of
the Dust, Out of Africa, Babette's Feast and Shirley
Valentine. Zora Neale Hurston, Maya Angelou and
Eleanor Roosevelt. Bill Moyers, Ellen Goodman and
Tom Friedman Secret Garden, Lyra and James Taylor.
Handel's Messiah and Mahler's Third Symphony.

I love knowing I have freedom and privacy
and safety,
faith in the Creator, confidence in the future,
people to love and people who love me,
challenges to meet
and opportunities to make a difference.

footnote: The word LOVE is used lavishly but not
without careful consideration. It is neither the love of
agape nor eros of which I speak. . . . It is the love that
makes the heart sing; the love of awe and appreciation; that which keeps the soul alive. . . .

Processing

When it's over, I want to say: all my life I was a bride married to amazement.
– Mary Oliver

Difficult times have helped me to understand better than before how infinitely rich and beautiful life is in every way.
– Isak Dinesen

The most remarkable thing about death is its insistence on harvesting life's meaning, even in those not prone to introspection.
– Joan Borysenko

One may not reach the dawn save by the path of the night.
– Kahlil Gibran

Your process writing probably will not appear in your spiritual-ethical will, but it may weave threads of your thoughts and feelings to help you shape your legacy document. Give yourself adequate time to reflect on and record your process. Here are some thoughts to ponder:

What was it like to write candidly, to move beyond your internal censor, to express what you love about your life and what you'll miss when you're gone? For me, the experience was bittersweet. I felt weepy immediately, aware that one day I would not be here enjoying this life. At the same time I felt incredibly fortunate to have a life full of beauty, love, and meaning.

Renowned author and psychotherapist, Irvin Yalom, poses the issue clearly: "What happens after we die is not really the problem. The challenge for us is how we live between now and then, whether we have the courage to stop denying it [death] and use our anxieties to live more authentic, meaning-filled and purposeful lives."

Consider ways you might use this exercise in your spiritual-ethical will. You may decide to include it just as it is, in your own handwriting (a powerful and unique way to be remembered), providing a snapshot for your loved ones of who you really are and what matters to you. It may include seeds for new blessings to plant for future generations. You may want it to be read by a loved one at your memorial service. It may suggest specific flowers you'd like at your grave site. For example, Vicki may want to have "fragrant springtime paper whites, freshly cut stately white tulips, white lilies and daisies" at her memorial service.

Reflect on your experience of the death and mourning rituals observed for your loved ones. Consider things you can do now to make those losses more emotionally or spiritually complete. How does the way death has been handled in your family or cultural group impact the choices you want to make regarding your own death?

Consider the significance of silence about death and dying. When does silence come from feelings and beliefs within you, and when from pressure from your family tradition and cultural habits? Are there death and dying situations when silence is preferable? What is the positive value of silence at a time of loss and grief? How has silence affected death practices in your life? What support do you need should you choose different rituals regarding your death? How can you include your preferences in your legacy document?

Writing my spiritual-ethical will was life changing for me. I began to experience myself and my life as precious. I realized that the way I approach my own dying process and how I ask to be treated at death is as important as any other thing I express to my children and grandchildren.

As habitual caretakers many women work tirelessly, hoping to deliver our loved ones from suffering and sadness. Until I went to Al-Anon, I had no clue about the impossibility of succeeding at this goal. Now I understand that our loved ones will be bereaved by our deaths, and they have the right, the need, and the responsibility to mourn their loss. The grieving process involves re-constructing a relationship which allows for a continuing and changing bond with the deceased.

Consider the consequences to a culture that avoids and denies death. All of us are affected; each of us is personally wounded, stripped of integrity and wholeness. Deprived of speaking our grief, we fail to honor our bonds with our ancestors. Other results include taking our life and its preciousness for granted. We live with the pretense and the false hope of limitlessness. As a result we are prone to procrastinate. Where is the urgency to do anything if we live as if we have forever? We make healthcare about cure, not care. When there's no cure, both the patient and the medical professionals fail. There's no place for acceptance of the reality of bodily death nor appropriate preparation for it. We neglect decisions and plans for the end of life – including writing a spiritual-ethical will – cheating future generations of our blessings, love, and wisdom.

I still grieve for the words unsaid. Something terrible happens when we stop the mouths of the dying before they are dead. A silence grows up between us then, profounder than the grave.
– Faye Moskowitz

The unexamined life is not worth living.
– Socrates

It is only past the meridian of fifty that one can believe that the universal sentence of death applies to oneself.
– May Sarton

Process Notes

Consider the value of putting your affairs in order. For those who feel anxious or overwhelmed thinking about death, there is a sense of accomplishment and an inner peace that comes with addressing death directly. (Note: If you are interested in additional reflections and writing about death and dying as well as practical and straightforward guidance for organizing the data of your life, preparing living wills, and wills of estate, see chapter 10, "Death and Dying" in *Women's Lives, Women's Legacies*.)

Keeping death secret limits awareness about life and our values. As humans we share the reality of death, though for each of us dying has a unique shape and meaning. We may be gentler than Jacob, blessing rather than instructing, asking rather than commanding, but it is appropriate to use the spiritual-ethical will to acknowledge mortality and express our preferences. We can request dignified treatment at the end of life. We can express wishes unique to our dying, funeral, burial. We can communicate how we want to be remembered after death. And we can, like Jacob, ask our family to honor those wishes after death.

How we approach and prepare for our own deaths, what we say and write and do, expresses our perspective about death, celebrates the preciousness of our lives, and is a sacred component of the spiritual-ethical will we leave our loved ones. It links us to our history and to the generations to come.

Facing our mortality inspires us to return to rituals of memory which deepen our connection with past generations. For example, in Jewish tradition the anniversary of parents' deaths are commemorated by burning a memorial candle and reciting the mourner's prayer.

In *To Begin Again,* author Naomi Levy speaks to our need for ritual especially at times of loss and death. "The religious rituals that our grandparents lived by have been all but forgotten. Many of our parents discarded them like an unwelcome inheritance . . . we who have been raised ritually naked yearn desperately to be wrapped in a mantle of meaning. We long for the structure, the holiness, and the shelter that rituals can provide. . . .

The legacy of frozen grief may affect offspring for generations to come.
– Pauline Boss

Tombstones mark time with eternity.
– Natalie Goldberg

Ritual involves taking time to understand how a certain facet of one's experience fits into the larger context of life.
– Denise Linn

"And so we find ourselves reaching out in an attempt to recover a birthright that has been discarded. . . . We are hungry for rituals because they transform mundane routines into sacred encounters and give us a way to express ourselves."

(Note: If you are interested in additional reflections and writing about rituals and the unique legacies that women have created honoring both life and death, I recommend the Ritual and Celebration sections in chapter 7, "A Woman's Spiritual Journey," and chapter 11, "Alternative Legacies," in *Women's Lives, Women's Legacies*.) Legacy writer, Sue Lewis, shares for your virtual legacy circle how she addressed her need for ritual when her mother died. Note how she transformed her personal need into a family legacy.

Memories of Mom

Prior to Mom's death she had established that she wished to be cremated, but she did not want a memorial service. Her cremains, boxed in a plain white cardboard box, were laid at temporary rest in mid-December on the top shelf in my brother's library. We would respectfully honor this loving woman in ways that would celebrate her unique spirit, but not immediately.

Her early lessons to my two brothers and me aimed to be practical, non-intrusive, and frugal. In this spirit we chose not to fly the family from all over the U.S. and Europe in the hectic month of December for a service she had requested not to have. We would gather instead at my brother's home in Iowa the next July. That would be a sensible time to celebrate – and heaven knows, we were taught to be sensible!

Yet needing an earlier closing ritual, I invited my siblings, children, uncles, and nephews to join me on Christmas afternoon to pause in each of our own spaces at 5:00 PM, Iowa time, light a candle and write reflections on how Mom had been a light in our lives. From Barcelona to California, from Vail to Florida, the warmth of our candles matched the warmth of our thoughts regarding this kind, gentle woman we celebrated.

The Christmas afternoon candlelight reflections are bound together as a family legacy. They are housed in my brother's library as a legacy to the family. It has been established as a central spot for our family archives as we all gather at the lake each July 4th.

My Mother's Hands . . .
by Sue McGuire

They cuddled and cradled me as a child . . .

They touched and held me when I was sad . . .

They taught me to stir and scrape the bowls for cooking . . .

They held my hot and sweaty head when I was ill . . .

They were often folded in prayer, praying for those far and near . . .

They clapped and congratulated when I did something well . . .

They pinned on my veil when I walked down the aisle . . .

They held my children with tenderness in her Bohemian style . . .

They kneaded and pounded the dough to make apple strudel . . .

They punched a hole in the dough for fruit-filled kalaches . . .

They massaged and trigger-pointed as she did her reflexology . . .

They caressed and coddled her great grandchild . . .

As her dementia took her memory – I returned the treasure of holding her hand . . .

I walk down the hall of her nursing home, hand in hand, guiding her to where she belongs . . .

Here is an excerpt of a woman's letter to her four grown children, written in 1981, not long after she'd been widowed. She kept the letter in her safety deposit box for twenty years. They read it sitting at her bedside as she lay dying. Imagine the love and healing shared by the five of them as they read together:

"My dearest children: No one knows how much time God has allotted to them and I can't leave you without a final word. I was never a very demonstrative person, but I have always loved you all very much and have been so proud of you . . . so do not mourn my passing beyond showing your respect for me. The important thing is how you treated me when I was alive – and that you couldn't have done better. I love you all and hope you all have many happy years with your families and friends and are able to realize all your hopes and dreams. Your loving Mother"

Your virtual legacy circle includes excerpts from legacy letters by two younger mothers. The first was written by a courageous mother to her adult son four years after his sister was killed in a car accident. The second was written by a mother to her incarcerated son. Notice especially the serenity inherent in the honest reflections and choices of these two women.

To close this chapter, I share a letter I wrote to my own daughter and granddaughters. In it I told them the story of my mother's death, passed on our tradition of women being the warriors, caring for mourners' families, and I closed the letter with a double blessing: words of blessing and a delicious recipe.

Loss is a magical preservative.
– Eva Hoffman

It's only when we truly know and understand that we have a limited time on earth – and we have no way of knowing when our time is up – that we will begin to live each day to the fullest, as if it was the only one we had.
– Elisabeth Kübler-Ross

Performing a ritual is like kissing God.
– Naomi Levy

To My Dear Son,

By the time you read this, I will be facing my mortality or I will have passed. In either case, I want to leave this message for you – my only son, and only surviving child. I want you to know what a distinct privilege it has been to be your mother and how much pride I have taken in watching you grow into the kind and loving man you've become. Indulge me one last time, by allowing me to impart some wisdom and advice that I want you to remember always. If we haven't spoken about my wishes concerning my burial, I will provide them for you in writing.

First of all, I want to be buried at Lakewood next to your sister. The plot is large enough for two coffins and a cremation vault. It doesn't much matter to me whether I'm cremated or placed in a coffin. If Dad passes before me, we'll allow him first choice. If I'm placed in a coffin my only preference is that the casket be closed. I don't want people looking at me, commenting on how natural I look, or not. I want people to remember me as I was. If I have a casket, please make it a simple oak one like your sister's. I'd like a spray of white flowers – roses, orchids and lilies on top. Keep the burial private, just immediate family.

Now that was the easy part. The remainder of this message will bring tears as I write them. . . .

Dear Vijay, my son,

Neither of us want to think about a time when the other is no longer here to do what we do so well, which is love each other. We worked hard for that chance, this lifetime. No one's life is without its element of non-normal, perfect storms, battering times. You and I know what this looks like, and sometimes we have to ask for the gift of humility when we get caught up in our righteous belief that we have had weird lives. We are not alone, you know. And when I am gone, you won't be alone, either. More about that later.

My dear, dear friend, _____, is executor of my estate. She knows where all my papers are and she has my legal permission to take care of things. I have left each of my loved ones with what I think will help them, to the best of my ability. Use my passing, and the resources that flow to you, as a time to STRENGTHEN the family, to STRENGTHEN yourself. May you be blessed with a generous heart that accepts your own treasure as *finally enough,* or perhaps even more than you expected. Humility brings gratefulness. Gratefulness is another way of saying "I am full. I have enough." May it visit you every day.

I think I would prefer to be cremated, although if this offends you or others whose thoughts and concerns are important to you, bury me. If so, I would prefer to be buried in the manner of Judaism, within 24 hours and without embalming, in a wooden casket. You can bury my ashes (or my body) where you wish, where it is convenient to you if you have an interest in visiting. Otherwise Lakewood in Minneapolis or Park View in Duluth are both good choices. Toss some ashes in the big lake at Brighton Beach, and in the woods up at Northern Pine. Make it a time to tell the best stories – my ferocious love of family, my silly humor, my propensity to fall down and forget names. . . .

Dear Carlin and Emily,

When I started to work with people who were dying, I know that there were periodic murmurs between you about how that was all that I thought about. But what I want you to know is that one of the primary reasons I love this work is that I have learned and have full permission to talk about what is essential with people who know that they don't have time.

When people get a life threatening illness, they are forced to cultivate and strengthen other parts of themselves if they choose to do the work of preparing to die and close their life with healing. While I know when I was your age I couldn't believe this, no matter what you do or what you eat, your body will disease, decay and die. There is no way to ward this off. I remember sitting in a workshop with Joan Halifax who said, "Everyone in this room is going to die." Even for me, after 15 years of working with people with life threatening illness, there was a slight startle in me – "even me" I thought to myself....

When I had pulmonary emboli two summers ago, just before your wedding, Carlin, and just as you got pregnant, Emily, I remember feeling an overwhelming sense of gratitude for making it through the condition. When I came home, I called many people, crying and thanking them for all they had done for me. As time went on, the intensity of that gratitude and love faded a bit. I have learned that looking at death is like looking at the sun. We look and turn away, look and turn away. We cannot sustain the gaze without getting burned. It is too much....

I know that wisdom is hard to pass on. But what I would most wish for you, Carlin and Emily, is that you work with the illusion that you have forever and be mindful of how you spend each day. May you find the joy of risking living with an open heart, of trying not to let the needs of your ego dictate your life, to cultivate a presence with whatever is real and true for you, pushing nothing away and not grasping at things, and finding the ease of living that comes with being willing to let your heart break open.....

Here is [an excerpt of] a poem that has been a guide to me in these last few years.

There is a cry deeper than all sound whose serrated edges
cut the heart as we break open to the place inside
which is unbreakable and whole, while learning to sing.
– Rashani

With love, Mom

Aunt Millie's Sweet Noodle Kugel

To my daughter and granddaughters:

I first tasted Millie's kugel at the meal following my mother's funeral on October 13, 1972. How well I remember that day – radiant sunshine and fluorescent yellow leaves clothed the triple-trunked birch tree at 11903 Hilloway Road.

Led by Aunt Millie, my mother's friends had arrived the day before – a swarming, loving cadre of women armed with coffeepots and serving trays. They checked my cupboards and refrigerator making lists of what was needed. I stood limp and helpless at the edge of my kitchen while they organized for shiva.

Aunt Millie, not really my aunt but a close family friend, was one of my mother's many female friends who loved me. She was affectionate, playful, cheerful, free-spirited. She often swore and broke other rules of the day about being ladylike.

I have spotty recall of those days in 1972, mostly because of the shock and numbness of early, unexpected grief. I waded through the minutes and hours as through a thick shroud of mist.

On Saturday, my father told me he hadn't known what to do, so he'd taken mother to the hospital. On Monday an arrest. Paddled back to life? Coma, high fever, strong antibiotics, kidney malfunction. Then at dusk on Wednesday, a resident, hiding an autopsy permission form on a clipboard behind his back, took Daddy and me to an airless space behind an elevator and pronounced my mother dead.

We left the hospital and went to a restaurant for dinner. I was starving, yet amazed that I could even think about eating at such a moment. Daddy and I sat across from each other, talking little. What was there to say? It felt bizarre then, and now, forty years later, it still does. I was a month short of turning thirty-five, and mother was two weeks short of fifty-seven. And she was dead.

I remember little of the funeral. Coming back from the cemetery was a shock. In my absence, the warrior women had transformed my living room with tables, set for forty or fifty people, heavily laden with the traditional post-funeral meal: hard-boiled eggs, bagels and cream cheese, tuna salad, cottage cheese, herring, and Aunt Millie's kugel.

The kugel was such a comfort as it went down – sweet and warm and solid – just what I needed to fortify me for the coming days when I would have to integrate this new reality: I no longer had a mother.

Honoring the dead honors life. I took great comfort in the power of shiva, in the many people who came to express their condolences and tell stories. They shared their version of Bea, Auntie Bea, surprising me with aspects of her I'd not known and loving her in ways impossible for me to have imagined. I found solace in the power of community sitting down to eat together after a burial, sharing foods symbolic of life. And I was strengthened by the power of women taking charge at a time of death – organizing, preparing, and serving food to mourners, nourishing bodies and spirits as a team of life-keepers.

As I have aged and taken my turn as a warrior woman, I have always volunteered to make the kugel, Aunt Millie's kugel. It is a tradition that keeps my memories – of my mother, her death, and her generation – alive. And it is a link to our tradition, binding us through death and life, generation to generation.

So I pass this kugel recipe down to you, my daughter and granddaughters, as part of my legacy. May you make this kugel when you become part of the cadre of women honoring the life of a beloved person who has died. Let it bring warm and solid sustenance to the survivors, helping them to mourn so they can return to life.

May Aunt Millie's kugel sweeten your lives and the lives of those you love.

NOODLE KUGEL
(In Aunt Millie's words, October 1972)

1 lb. wide egg noodles (boil according to directions; rinse with cold water)

Add: 1 quart buttermilk
        1/4 lb. melted butter or margarine
        1/2 C. sugar
        Salt – "How much? A nice teaspoonful"
        6 eggs (well beaten)

Throw all together – eggs last – sprinkle 1/2 C. Parmesan cheese on top.
Bake in 350° oven for 1 to 1 1/2 hours.

*May your
spiritual-ethical will
link you and those you
love for eternity*

CHAPTER FIVE

$\mathcal{B}$reaking the Silence

Legacy Letters

By the 12th century the traditional ethical will had taken the form of a written letter. In it men transmitted values to their sons. Their purpose was to impart ethical and moral instruction to assure continuity of their culture from one generation to next. They also specified children's responsibilities related to burying and mourning their father.

To bring us from the 12th to the twenty-first century, I quote myself from the introduction to *Women's Lives, Women's Legacies*. Writing a spiritual-ethical will is "a natural undertaking for women today. We are the weavers, the storytellers, the memory vessels who gather, build, and sustain our communities. Regardless of our religious beliefs, the spiritual-ethical will is a powerful tool for unleashing our voices, power, and purpose.

"At this precarious moment in history, we realize that life is fragile and we do not control the number of our days. Many of us feel a sense of urgency, a need to document our legacies and raise our voices to help shape this

May the Creator who dwells in all things fill you with love and light and peace. May you provide shade, beauty, and healing for all who come in contact with you.

– Denise Linn

Our spiritual and religious lives depend on the stories we choose to tell and how we tell them.

– Sandy Eisenberg Sasso

unfolding new world. We have an obligation to record our personal values and family stories. In so doing, we strengthen the fabric of civilization."

Remember we began with the understanding that legacy work is part self-discovery and expression, and part expressing our wisdom and love for the benefit of future generations. It is legitimate to address both in your legacy letters to your loved ones.

Know that your needs – to belong, to be witnessed, to be remembered, to have your life make a difference, to bless and be blessed and to celebrate life – all have a place in your legacy. When we wrote about the legacies of our foremothers in chapter 1, we also addressed our own need to belong, to be connected to a rich personal and cultural history. We discovered in chapter 2 that domesticity, long ignored or demeaned, is a powerful and worthy part of our feminine essence. Witnessing it in ourselves and in others makes us more wholly-holy feminine. We added our souls to the blessings we wrote in chapter 3. That snapshot of who we are and what we value makes the blessing more authentic and welcomed by your loved ones. (See the Appendix for a legacy letter template, pages 126-128.) It also addresses our need to be remembered. When we considered mortality in chapter 4, we gave ourselves permission, with the encouragement of Elisabeth Kübler-Ross, to express what we want in relation to our own dying and death. That expression, which models our unique perspective about the preciousness of life and death, is a tangible way for our lives to make a difference.

Dear Descendants,

If I had my life to live over again, I would like to take more time to listen to others rather than spending time defending my point of view. I would be sillier and more willing to make a fool of myself. I wouldn't take life so seriously, and I would laugh a lot more, especially at myself. I would push myself to take more risks. I would love my body no matter what shape it was in, and I wouldn't apologize for things that had nothing to do with me.

I would love deeply and fully without fear of rejection. I would be kind to people for no reason, without ever expecting anything in return. I would forgive myself instantly rather than carry guilt and recrimination. I wouldn't be in such a hurry; I would relax more, have more fun, spend more time with friends, dance in the rain, and sing out loud to my heart's content, even if I couldn't carry a tune.

Perhaps, dear descendants, these are things that you learn only after living life, but if my experiences can help you in the smallest way, it will make the struggles that I have gone through so much easier to bear. I believe in you. I have seen you in my dreams and my visions. You have my love. I will continue to send you my love through time and space.

Your Ancestor,
Denise

(Denise Linn in *Sacred Legacies*)

Here we are, finished with all the preparation and ready to write our legacies. You can be confident about your writing skills and material to include. You've reflected, visualized using your intuition, written exercises and process notes, and witnessed offerings and letters by women in your virtual legacy circle. You've gathered history, perspectives, and values about who you are and what matters to you.

I admit my failure to keep my promise that you would write your spiritual-ethical will within two hours. I apologize. We're out of time! But you've come this far, and you're prepared. Will you commit just fifteen more minutes?

You've examined your history and harvested legacies from your foremothers; you've explored and come to a new appreciation – surprise, surprise – of the domestic aspect of your femininity; you've learned to transform instructions into blessings, you've even contemplated your own death and how your mortality will influence your legacy.

We need just fifteen (15) minutes more to write a legacy letter to someone you love. "Fifteen minutes," you say, laughing, "why that's impossible!" I counter your doubt with a true story.

The first time I asked women in a legacy circle to write a fifteen minute legacy letter, it was for homework during the week between two circle meetings. One woman came to the circle exactly fifteen minutes late. She explained that she'd conveniently not made time to write during the week. But when she got to the door, she felt embarrassed, and timing herself, wrote a letter while she sat in her car. When she read it to the circle, women nodded with appreciation. Her letter was proof that when we trust that we have something to say, have the courage to express it, and have our hearts open to our loved ones, the writing comes easily and elegantly!

Of course, each of our spiritual-ethical wills will be unique. For many of us one fifteen minute legacy letter will be adequate or even perfect. Some women may decide that each loved one deserves a letter of her or his own. Others of you may decide that this has been a good introduction, but that you want to continue writing, perhaps gathering your own circle of support. Or you may decide to add to your spiritual-ethical will, writing new letters each Thanksgiving, New Year, or on the occasions of your loved ones' or your own special birthdays, graduations, and weddings.

Some of you may choose to write an empty-nest book like Susan Strassfeld's *Everything I Know,* a gift for her daughter when she left for college. (If you're interested in writing about your purpose for gifting things as part of your legacy, see "My Most Valuable Possessions" in chapter 8, of *Women's Lives, Women's Legacies.*)

Women whose unique talents are visual, artistic, or in various crafts may want to include other mediums such as photographs, quilts, stitchery, or scrapbooks. (Suggestions and examples in chapter 11, "Alternative Legacies," in *Women's Lives, Women's Legacies* can guide you.)

Some women find legacy letters an opportunity to share their thoughts about their financial legacies. (Chapter 9, "Women's Financial Legacies," in *Women's Lives, Women's Legacies* also addresses philanthropic gifts and a guide for choosing and working with an estate planner to create your legal will.)

Considering Content for Your Legacy Letter

Our goal now is to write one fifteen-minute letter. Begin with chapter 1 to consider material to include in your legacy letter.

Review the list of questions about what you wanted to know about your feminine ancestor. As those questions opened a window into her life, you might now consider them a mirror into your own. These may be the very questions that future generations will want to know about you!

Reread the letter your foremother wrote to you and review the topics and values she addressed to you. You may or may not want to pass these on to future generations in your family.

Recall the midrash you wrote in chapter 1: the letter that gave Dina of

We each have the power to take all the richness of our past with us, to carry it into the uncertain future.
– *Naomi Levy*

People become the stories they hear and the stories they tell.
– *Elie Wiesel*

Our lives extend beyond our skins, in radical interdependence with the rest of the world.
– *Joanna Macy*

Never doubt that a small group of committed citizens can change the world: Indeed it's the only thing that ever has.
– *Margaret Mead*

Genesis a voice. If what you wrote for Dina is relevant to you today, you may want to include it as part of your legacy to both genders in the next generations of your family.

Re-evaluate your respect for the sanctity of the home and the meaning inherent in homemaking. Recall Hestia's spiritual legacy to women, examined in chapter 2. Contemplate breaking the silence and sharing what you discovered about your feminine nature in your spiritual-ethical will.

Reread the instructions that you received from your foremothers, listed in chapter 3. Weigh carefully the instructions that you chose to bless your loved ones with. Consider the blessing you wrote, and other instructions awaiting transformation into blessings. Blessings express your values, life lessons, hard-won wisdom, and love. They can be central themes in your legacy letter.

Revisit your responses to *What I love about my life is . . .* and *What I'll miss when I'm gone is . . .* in chapter 4. Clarifying gratitude for your life and articulating preferences about your death may help your loved ones to understand you. Be sure to include personal reasons for your requests. A legacy writer who wanted her organs and tissue donated to science at her death was concerned that her children would resist her wish. In her legacy letter, she expressed what she wanted and concluded with: "Although it may be hard for you, please understand and respect my choice. This decision is about my life making a difference, and my death a gift. My donation will make prolonged and healthier life possible for people in need."

Writing Legacy Letters

When you've completed your review, refill your tea cup or coffee mug, get comfortable in your favorite chair, set your timer for fifteen minutes, pick up your pen and write a legacy letter to a loved one. When you're finished, write some process notes, and set your letter aside for at least a day.

Date of writing:

My dear _____ , I want to tell you . . . _____

_____

_____

_____

_____

_____

_____

_____

_____

_____

_____

_____

_____

_____

_____

Process Notes

Editing Your Legacy Letter

Should you decide to edit your letter, there follows a page for your use. As has been consistent throughout the workbook, I caution about undue concern regarding grammar and punctuation.

Legacy work is neither about perfection, nor readying a manuscript for publication. Conversely, it has always been about two things: finding your voice to express your authentic self, and understanding the importance of passing on your wisdom and your love to a world sorely in need of both.

Reread your legacy letter after you and it have rested, providing you with the distance that provides perspective. Here are some thoughts for your editing consideration:

You may question whether to be wholly honest as you express who you are, whether to express old resentments or anger, whether to share family secrets that have been passed down as negative legacies, or to protect yourself and others by remaining silent.

There is no one right answer. Each of us must weigh what we write on scales unique to our situation, family, and tradition. The Buddha's wisdom for living "do no harm" is an excellent guide for your decisions about tone and what to include or exclude in your letter. But no matter how careful you are, there is no guarantee that your letter will be received in the way you intend. The best you can do is be honest with yourself and trust that what you've written is honest, ethical, and loving; you must be willing to let go of the outcome.

Another consideration is the appropriate time to present your letter. Should you, like the widow in chapter 4, write your letter and put it safely away to assure that the earliest it will be read is at the time of your death? Some of you will prefer dialogue with its potential of changing relationships with your loved ones as a result of your legacy letter. Each of us will have unique reasons for our decision in this regard.

Not to reveal yourself to another is never to believe the real you is worth loving.
– Gail Whiting

In every deliberation, we must consider the impact of our decisions on the next seven generations.
– From The Great Law of the American Indian Iroquois Confederacy

Women's written words will change the culture.
– Joan Drury

Write down all the stuff you swore you'd never tell another soul. Remember that you own what happened to you.
– Anne Lamott

To write is to sow and to reap at the same time.
– Ruth Brin*

Life is all about getting our story straight and passing it along in all its street-smart wisdom to the next generation.
– Lawrence A. Hoffman*

If you do decide to communicate your letter in the present or near future, be sure that you prepare your loved ones. One legacy writer mailed copies of her letter to her children living all across the globe, without any preparation. They called her, anxious and distraught, fearing that her letter was her way of telling them she had a dread disease and was announcing her imminent death. She was surprised that she'd gotten neither the desired nor the expected response to her letter of love.

Finally, edit your letter as you did your blessing in chapter 3. Check that you've conveyed the messages you want your loved ones to have. Use words that clarify what you want understood and that sound like you. Make sure that your tone is consistent with your message. Consider the energy your letter will carry fifty or a hundred years from today. Imagine that you are the recipient of the letter; how does it feel to receive this gift? Read the letters shared in your virtual legacy circle. Use them in any way that helps you express yourself, your values, blessings, and wisdom. Break any rules you've read here to make your letter your own!

Date of edit:

My dear _____ , _____

Excerpts from Legacy Letters

Bless yourself with forgiveness, dear one. I wish for you the peace that comes with forgiving those who couldn't love you enough, those who hurt you nearly beyond repair, and those who helped but couldn't fix everything.

I know your love for me. Know that my love for you never ends. Love me back every day as you do the right things, the simple things, the things that bring people and love into your life. Love me back every day when you show your children-to-be the best of their lovely, sweet papa. I have loved you more than my own skin. Love yourself now, with this same ferocity.

My sincerest hope is that you will use the foundation we have tried to provide and then take off to build a structure that has never been imagined before – uniquely you – that will blow the world's socks off! I will always love you both with all my heart and soul.

Dear daughter (two days after her wedding) . . .

You were a glowing, gorgeous, and gracious bride. He was a handsome, wholesome, and honorable groom . . . it was an honor and privilege to walk beside you along with your father to present and accompany you to the man you so love – your soul mate. He is a fine and faithful man. . . .

May you both always honor and respect your uniqueness and individuality along with your oneness in becoming husband and wife.

My legacy for you, daughter, is that you may always honor and respect your oneness and at the same time delight in who you are, and who your mate is. Never lose your spark and energy that glows from you. May you find the love you have always hoped for. May you know patience, compromise, communication, and abiding love in your life together. May laughter twinkle in your being and may joy be in your heart. May the Holy One richly bless your life together. Lovingly, your Mother

My wonderful first Granddaughter –

I was so excited when you were born. I went out and bought you a red and white smocked dress and a pair of red patent leather shoes. One of the dolls I made for you is now wearing those clothes. I held you and rocked you and sent you all the love I could.

I have watched you grow into a beautiful, talented young woman.

I know a granddaughter never likes to hear that she is like her grandmother, but I see in you so much of myself at your age. Even our left-handedness and our kinky hair.

I worry about you – my heart aches wishing I could protect you. I know that I can't. I can be there for you if you will let me. I understand a great deal of your pain. I am aware of the conflict in your home. I am aware of situations you are faced with, situations that no child should ever have to deal with.

I want you to know I had a father who was an alcoholic and suffered much of the same hurt and pain you are experiencing.

I would like to bless you with the ability to be strong and insightful. May you have the strength to be able to see that none of what is happening is your fault. Your mother and father have their own hurts from their growing up experiences.

I bless you with the ability to know what a wonderful young woman you are and how much you are loved. I stand on the sidelines willing to be called in at any time for any reason.

With love, Your Grandmother

To my daughters:

Because I love you both so much, I want to pass along to you what I believe in and what guides me. . . . *Tikkun olam* is the centerpiece of living a Jewish life. My own method of "healing the world" was to become a social worker and to try to help heal people's pain one soul at a time. What a wonderful world we would have if each of us would strive to leave it better than it was left to us.

Here is what I hope for you both as women: I hope I've conveyed to you a sense of how strong, intelligent and capable you are. I so respect your talents; I hope you also respect them. Just as important is that we all respect the boundaries of others and insist that our own are respected.

I have watched admiringly as you both have faced obstacles in the world and, with courage, overcome them. Always expect the best of yourselves and of others; the world and you are deserving of no less. . . .

I take more pride in being your mother than in anything else I've done in my life. I wish for the two of you unconditional acceptance and friendship [as sisters] as you make your journeys through life.

To close this very somber statement of my values: Life is uncertain – eat dessert first! My love always, Mom

My dear first son –

I have been writing about the legacy of the fractured family; I come from one and you do too. It is something I didn't want to pass on to you – hoped I wouldn't. . . .

I know what it is like to feel orphaned and abandoned. I always hoped to be adopted by someone – some family; my in-laws, your in-laws. I can understand your longing to be part of your wife's family. . . .

I hope you will be blessed with a beautiful, unfractured family, one that you create with your wife and will be able to pass on as a legacy. May you love your children devotedly and joyfully and may they return this love, nurturing you until your heart is full and each empty place cries out with joy and happiness.

Forgive me, my son, for my imperfections as a mother; forgive me for not meeting all your needs. I had such dreams of creating a happy family and I was so often tired and worried and working too hard. Be happy, my darling

My dear son,

I have lived my life to show you the value of community. As an only child myself I watched my parents live their lives giving to others and bringing good into their friendships. Sometimes they were so needy that I as the child cared for them. I learned that I became more full by giving out. But it is also crucial to receive.

So as you grew out of my arms and into your bike, into school friends and biking buddies, and then into driving your car, I watched you grow into your full self. My heart sings at your decisions to trust in yourself.

Even in my worried moments, or my sadness at being more on the outer corners of your developing life, I love you. I have quietly sent you to seek your life.

Do not perceive my distance as any lack of love. Without the deep love, faith and blessing I feel from your passage through my life I would be mere dust.

It is a love that you opened in my heart that will never die. Always we are connected and true to one another.

May you feel my love as it lingers and nurtures your heart. It is the base you stand on. May you be fearless in sharing this love with others. And, even if they simply pass through, let the love you feel keep you open.

When your heart aches with loss, change, sadness, even fear, return to our love: mother to son. I love you always and forever, Your Mom

Dearest son,

I am watching you from afar as you start your life after college. It is an exciting moment for me to see more and more of you emerging, to watch you making your choices, solving your problems, meeting new people, building your life. I am happy that you are sharing so much with us, but I am happy that you are living your life.

I have written many pieces to you in these three years since your brother died. Few you have seen, but they are for you with the hope you will know me better and can come to know my thoughts, even things I consider my secrets. I will feel good if I believe you have known me, your mother, fully.

Today as I write, I wish you a life without secrets. I hope you can share your deep sides, your private thoughts, your hard stuff with your friends and the women you come to love. I believe so strongly that secrets separate us from others and take up space inside us. I believe that I lived a life using energy, holding hidden things I had done that I wasn't proud of. I tried to raise you and your brother in an environment where all subjects could be discussed: alcohol, mistakes, dishonesty, death. I am proud of my efforts to turn things around and make different the family atmosphere which I knew, where there wasn't openness and where mistakes were criticized.

So I wish you a life where your secrets need not stay hidden, where your relationships are never separated by secrets, and where you can be open and close with those you love.

With all my love and respect, Mom

You've reached the end of this workbook with its reflections and exercises. Congratulations on completing your first legacy letter . . . and may it be just one of many that you write to your loved ones, family, friends, and communities.

May your experience of writing your spiritual-ethical will be well received by those you love. May your words fill holes in their hearts and gaps in their histories.

Imagine the influence the gift of your life, your history, your values and blessings may have beyond today: twenty, fifty, even a hundred years from now. You have contributed to a world that yearns for women's wisdom. Celebrate that you are part of a broad community of women whose voices and courage will impact future generations in ways unknowable, so that they, like you, will be blessed with roots and a feminine history to nurture them in the years ahead.

I am both humbled and empowered by this sacred work, and grateful to have participated in it with you. Thank you. May your spiritual-ethical will link you eternally with those who came before, those for whom you care, and unborn generations.

No seed ever sees the flower.
– Zen koan

We are all meant to shine, as children do. And as we let our own light shine, we unconsciously give other people permission to do the same.
– Marianne Williamson

May God keep you safe 'til the word of your life is fully spoken.
– Anonymous Irish blessing

Appendix

Template for Writing a One-Page Legacy Letter and a Sample Letter

By the 12th century the traditional ethical will, men transmitting values to their sons, had taken the form of a written letter. Writing ethical wills is a natural undertaking for women today. We are the concerned storytellers who build, maintain and sustain family, community, and civilization.

Each of our ethical wills is unique. For many women a one-page legacy letter will be adequate or even perfect. Others may decide that each of her loved ones deserves a letter of their own. Still other women may continue to write legacy letters for a variety of purposes, to:
- commemorate special occasions, holidays or special birthdays
- express gratitude and celebrate life
- provide family history
- express values, love and blessings
- share life lessons, successes, regrets, disappointments
- tell the story of precious possessions
- make amends, ask forgiveness, share secrets
- request preferences for end-of-life care and ways to be remembered
- explain decisions in our legal documents: health directives, wills

I usually suggest that writers use timers, and limit writing to fifteen minutes, an amount of time that demands focus but is not so lengthy that one can excuse themselves with "not having the time". Women are always amazed at what can be accomplished in so short a time. Their amazement surprises me when we are so accomplished as multi-taskers!

Whatever the content, a template provides a structure to make writing legacy letters easier. A one page fifteen minute letter can be accomplished in four paragraphs.

Paragraph 1: Provide history and context. One of my mentors once said, "All texts have a context." We are seldom aware that the context beyond our personal lives affects us. The time when family history was contained in a family Bible and passed down from generation to generation is long gone. An opening paragraph to give the reader a snippet of family history and a snapshot of the historical times enriches what follows.

Paragraph 2: Tell the story. All of us have a sacred story, and all of us want to tell our stories. We feel known and have a sense of belonging when others listen attentively to our stories.

Paragraph 3: State the lesson learned. Learning from our experience is often defined as wisdom. It's this learning that we want to preserve and pass forward to future generations along with our love.

Paragraph 4: Offer a blessing. Your blessing flows naturally to your loved ones from your story and your learning. We're not always aware of the importance of being blessed, but we all need blessings from our elders. The ancient ethical will was born out of the story of Jacob blessing his twelve sons (though not his daughter, Dina) as he lay dying at the end of the book of Genesis. That same Jacob earlier stole his father Isaac's blessing from his older brother, Esau. Esau's response was a plea to his father, in my opinion the most poignant words in Genesis: (27:38) "Have you but one blessing, my father? Bless me, even me also…. And Esau lifted up his voice and wept."

Women too have the power to bless future generations. We're no different today. All of us need to be blessed, in our modern day, and as adults. We never outgrow our need for blessings! We experience being blessed as we bless future generations.

Here is a sample using the template: context, story, learning, blessing. I wrote this letter to my grown children after I read somewhere about "looking into people's faces when you pass them," that prompted a memory of my 1961 experience.

Dear Sid and Debbie,

In the summer of 1961, your Dad graduated from Officers Candidate School and began three years of service in the US Coast Guard. He was stationed at the Battery, at the south end of Manhattan. We sublet a ground-floor apartment on West 95th Street just half a block from Central Park in Spanish Harlem. At 22, I was optimistic, confident, and naively fearless. My job that summer was to find a teaching position for the fall.

One day on my way to some exciting adventure in the city, I got on the subway. I sat down and began to read. A pregnant, homeless woman entered the car, and began to beg for money. I averted my eyes, buried my face in my book, and clasped my heart and my purse tightly. Silent minutes passed and suddenly the woman began to shout at the riders – crying out that it was okay if we didn't give her money, but it wasn't okay to avoid looking her in the face – that she was a human being! She picked up her bags and lurched through the door into the next train car.

I was shocked and shamed. Since then, even when I choose not to give to a person begging, I look the person in the eye. I feel more human when I acknowledge another's humanity.

So, my beloved and precious children, Sid and Debbie, May you both be blessed with compassionate and wise eyes: eyes that see beyond the face of circumstance, that see the spark of the Divine deep within yourself, each other, and and everyone on our planet.

I love you, Mom

Bibliography

Angelou, Maya. *Letter to My Daughter.* NY: Random House, 2008.

Baines, Barry K., MD. *Ethical Wills: Putting Your Values on Paper.* San Francisco: Da Capo Press, Perseus Books Group, 2002, Second Edition, 2006.

The Bible. Revised Standard Edition. NY: American Bible Society, 1952.

Bolen, Jean Shinoda, MD. *Goddesses in Older Women.* NY: HarperCollins, 2001.

———. *The Millionth Circle: How to Change Ourselves and the World: The Essential Guide to Women's Circles.* Berkeley, CA: Conari, 1999.

Brookfield, Stephen D. *Becoming a Critically Reflective Teacher.* San Francisco: Jossey-Bass, 1995.

Eve, Nomi. *The Family Orchard.* NY: Alfred A. Knopf, 2000.

Falk, Marcia. *The Book of Blessings.* San Francisco: HarperSanFrancisco, 1996.

Freed, Rachael. *Women's Lives, Women's Legacies: Passing Your Beliefs and Blessings to Future Generations,* Second Edition. Minneapolis: MinervaPress, 2012.

Fremont, Helen. *After Long Silence.* NY: Delta, Delacorte Press, 1999.

Gafni, Marc. *Soul Prints: Your Path to Fulfillment.* NY: Fireside, Simon & Schuster, 2002.

Geller, Laura. "Encountering the Divine Presence." From *Four Centuries of Jewish Women's Spirituality: A Sourcebook.* Boston: Beacon Press, 1992.

Glückel of Hameln. *The Memoirs of Glückel of Hameln.* Marvin Lowenthal, translator. NY: Schocken Books, 1977.

Goldberg, Natalie. *Writing Down the Bones.* Boston: Shambhala, 1986.

Heilbrun, Carolyn G. *Writing a Woman's Life.* NY: Ballantine Books, 1988.

Herman, Judith, MD. *Trauma and Recovery.* NY: BasicBooks/Perseus, 1997.

Hoffman, Lawrence A. *The Journey Home.* Boston: Beacon Press, 2002.

Kaplan, Deborah; Siegal, B.; Laskin, Diana; et. al. *The New Growing Older: Women Aging with Knowledge and Power.* NY: Touchstone Books, 1994.

Leider, Richard J. *The Power of Purpose: Find Meaning, Live Longer, Better.* San Francisco: Berrett-Koehler, Second Edition, 2010.

Leider, Richard J. and David Shapiro. *Something to Live For: Finding Your Way in the Second Half of Life.* San Francisco: Berrett-Koehler, 2008.

L'Engle, Madeleine. *Herself: Reflections on a Writing Life.* Compiled by Carole F. Chase. Colorado Springs, CO: Shaw Books (WaterBrook Press), 2001.

Laurence, Margaret. *The Stone Angel.* NY: Alfred A. Knopf, 1964.

Lessing, Doris. *The Summer before the Dark.* NY: Vintage Books, 1973.

Levy, Naomi. *Talking to God.* NY: Doubleday, 2002.

————. *To Begin Again: The Journey Toward Comfort, Strength, and Faith in Difficult Times.* NY: Alfred A. Knopf, 1998.

Linn, Denise. *Sacred Legacies: Healing Your Past and Creating a Positive Future.* NY: Random House, Ballantine Publishing Group, 1998.

Nouwen, Henri. *Life of the Beloved: Spiritual Living in a Secular World.* NY: The Crossroad Publishing Company, 1992.

Perlman, Debbie. *Flames to Heaven: New Psalms for Healing & Praise.* Wilmette, Illinois: RadPublishers, 1998.

Piercy, Marge. *The Art of Blessing the Day.* NY: Alfred A. Knopf, 1999.

————. *My Mother's Body.* NY: Alfred A. Knopf, 1985.

Pipher, Mary, PhD. *Another Country: Navigating the Emotional Terrain of Our Elders.* NY: Riverhead Books, 1999.

Plaskow, Judith, and Carol P. Christ, editors. *Weaving the Visions: New Patterns in Feminist Spirituality.* San Francisco: HarperSanFrancisco, 1989.

Remen, Rachel Naomi. *Kitchen Table Wisdom.* NY: Riverhead Books, 1996.

————. *My Grandfather's Blessings.* NY: Riverhead Books, 2000.

Rich, Adrienne. *On Lies, Secrets, and Silence.* NY: W. W. Norton & Company, 1979.

Roiphe, Anne. *Generation without Memory.* NY: The Linden Press/Simon & Schuster, 1981.

Scott-Maxwell, Florida. *The Measure of My Days.* NY: Penguin Books, 1979.

Sheehy, Gail. *New Passages: Mapping Your Life across Time.* NY: Random House, 1995.

Spangler, David. *Blessing: The Art and the Practice.* NY: Riverhead Books, 2001.

Strassfeld, Susan. *Everything I Know: Basic Life Rules from a Jewish Mother.* NY: Scribner, 1998.

Taylor, Daniel. *Creating a Spiritual Legacy: How to Share Your Stories, Values, and Wisdom.* Grand Rapids, MI: Brazos Press, 2011.

———. *Letters to My Children: A Father Passes on His Values.* Downers Grove, Ill.: InterVarsity Press, 1989.

Tornstam, Lars, Ph.D. *Gerotranscendence.* New York: Springer Publishing Company, 2005.

———. "Maturing Into Gerotranscendence," *The Journal of Transpersonal Psychology.* Vol. 43, No. 2, pp. 166-180, 2011.

Turnbull, Susan B. *The Wealth of Your Life: A Step-by-Step Guide for Creating Your Ethical Will.* Wenham, MA: Benedict Press, 2005, Second Edition, 2007, Third Edition, 2012.

Tyrrell, Mary. *Become a Memoirist for Elders.* St. Paul, MN: Memoirs, Inc., 2012.

Index

Legacy Programs

Rachael Freed is available to facilitate programs, retreats, and legacy workshops for groups, organizations, and faith communities. For more information contact her at 612-558-3331 or Rachael@life-legacies.com

Facilitating Legacy Circles

For information about facilitating legacy circles, contact Rachael at 612-558-3331 or Rachael@life-legacies.com

Other Legacy Resources

Women's Lives, Women's Legacies ~ Passing Your Beliefs and Blessings to Future Generations: Creating Your Own Ethical Will.
Minneapolis: MinervaPress, 2005, Second Edition 2012.

Legacy Tips&Tools (free monthly e-news) Subscribe at www.life-legacies.com

Coming in 2013: (working title)
Your Legacy Matters:
Harvesting the Love and Lessons of Your Life
~ An Intergenerational Guide for Creating Your Ethical Will ~

A Call to Readers/Legacy Writers

You are invited to submit your writing for inclusion on the life-legacies web site or in future legacy publications.

Consider submitting your letters ending your foremother's and Dina's silence, your description of a meaningful domestic activity, your instructions and blessings, your legacy letters on any topic.

Please provide a copy of this invitation filled out completely via email, with one attached copy of your writing as a Word document.

If your writing or an excerpt from it is chosen for inclusion online or in a future publication, you will receive confirmation prior to publication.

Thank you in advance for joining the virtual women's legacy circle!

How I want to be acknowledged for my contribution:
- ❏ not acknowledged (anonymous)
- ❏ my name with my contribution
- ❏ my name alphabetically as a contributor only in the general acknowledgements

My name (print it as you wish it to appear): _____

Please PRINT legibly:
Name _____
Address _____
_____ (zip/postal code) _____
Phone #: _____ Cell # _____
E-mail address: _____
(Please update your email address by emailing Rachael@life-legacies.com)

CPSIA information can be obtained
at www.ICGtesting.com
Printed in the USA
BVHW022128080223
658184BV00004B/43